THE PATHWAY to *Transcendent* PEACE

ROBYN AND BRANDI CUNNINGHAM

The Pathway to Transcendent Peace
Copyright 2023 by Robyn and Brandi Cunningham
Published by Robyn and Brandi Cunningham

All rights reserved. No part of this book may be reproduced, stored in a retrieval system, or transmitted in any form or by any means—electronic, mechanical, photocopy, recording, or otherwise—without prior written permission of the copyright owner. The names of some people in this book have been changed to protect their identity.

Unless otherwise noted, all Scripture quotations are from the Amplified Bible (AMP): Scripture taken from the Amplified® Bible, Copyright © 1954, 1958, 1962, 1964, 1965, 1987 by the Lockman Foundation Used by Permission. (www.Lockman.org)

Scripture quotations marked (ESV) are from The ESV® Bible (The Holy Bible, English Standard Version®), copyright © 2001 by Crossway, a publishing ministry of Good News Publishers. Used by permission. All rights reserved.

Scriptures marked (NKJV) are taken from the NEW KING JAMES VERSION (NKJV): Scripture taken from the NEW KING JAMES VERSION®. Copyright© 1982 by Thomas Nelson, Inc. Used by permission. All rights reserved.

Scripture quotations marked (KJV) are from the King James Version and are in the public domain.

Scripture quotations marked (NIV) taken from The Holy Bible, New International Version® NIV® Copyright © 1973, 1978, 1984, 2011 by Biblica, Inc. Used with permission. All rights reserved worldwide.

All emphasis in Scripture is the author's own.

ISBNs: 978-1-953143-03-7 (paperback)
        978-1-953143-04-4 (digital)

Printed in the U.S.A.

This book is dedicated to Joyce Meyer, who taught me how to enjoy everyday life.

And to my husband and children, for having patience while I grow in the fruit of the spirit

To my children, may their adult lives and future family lives be filled with peace every single day.

Contents

Introduction	7
Chapter 1: Community Crime is a Result of Individual State of Being	11
Chapter 2: Peace-Robbing Behaviors	27
Chapter 3: How To Get Out of the Cycle	39
Chapter 4: Self-Sabotaging Tendencies	53
Chapter 5: Regaining Control Through Peace	65
Chapter 6: Recognizing and Getting Our Needs Met in Christ	75
Chapter 7: What Is Nurturing, and Why Is It So Important?	85
Chapter 8: What Is Meditation?	99
Chapter 9: Peace Scriptures for Soaking	109

Introduction

Did you know that you can train yourself to constantly remain in a place of perfect peace? You can experience peace and joy in your life on a daily basis; not just when you're in worship or when you're in the place you feel safest. It is interesting that, scientifically, we can create neuropathways that go toward certain areas in our brains. The more neuropathways we create going toward a specific area, the faster and more efficiently we can access that area. This is one reason God emphasized meditation so much in the Bible. We literally transform our brains to look like His *when we think on the things He thinks about*!

In a society that struggles to overcome stressors of all kinds—including anxiety, fear, confusion, and anger—the Lord very clearly put it on my heart to write this book to help guide people into peace using biblical principles. I want to get this information out to *everyone!* I *know* that the information I share right here, right now, is going to set you and many others free from everything that holds you back from total immersion in the peace of the Lord! For too long, Satan has kept us from being consistently in the place of peace that surpasses all understanding. I know that the struggle is real. No matter where you are at in your daily walk, I want to affirm you. You are doing a great job. You are doing enough. I bless you with the ability to find and remain in the peace of Jesus that makes you whole and ushers you into transcendent peace! I look forward to hearing your

The Pathway to Transcendent Peace

testimony of overcoming, entering into His peace, and remaining there consistently!

When we enter into the peace of the Lord that surpasses understanding, all of our other needs will be met.

- Everything falls into place
- We feel fulfilled
- We know who we are
- We operate from a place of wholeness—peace is a place of wholeness. Many of us are familiar with the word "shalom," which means peace.

It is my deepest heart's desire to see you walk in the fullness of everything the Lord Jesus has called you to walk in, and I'm going to help you do that through this book! If you are struggling with any of the following, this is for you:

- Anxiety
- Fear
- Inability to consistently remain in a place of perfect peace
- Worry
- Grief
- Loss
- Fear of rejection
- Fear of disconnection from people
- People-pleasing
- Anger
- Irritation
- Confusion
- Not knowing if you are in the right place at the right time
- Taking matters into your own hands when injustices are done to you (I think we're all guilty of this at some point—some of us more often than others)

Introduction

Throughout this book, you will:

- Recognize behaviors that rob you of peace
- Understand why certain things in your life have been recurring issues
- Get healing from those things
- Know how to get your needs met in Christ and be fulfilled
- Learn what it means to be nurtured and to nurture, and why that is so important
- Learn about biblical meditation and how to do it righteously
- Rewire your entire life to become a picture of Jesus
- Learn to live in the peace of God that surpasses all understanding by soaking in scriptures that pertain to peace

This journey is *not* for the faint of heart. It is very in-depth. It requires you to be fully engaged and completely honest. You only get as much out of something as you put into it. I pray you stop here and determine in your heart that you are *committed* to doing whatever it takes to wholeheartedly seek the shalom peace of the Lord.

I'm SO excited to share this because it is the answer to many people's interpersonal relationship issues and problems. It is the answer to finding peace in every area of your life—your walk with God, your walk with yourself, and your walk with others.

> *I pray over every person reading this book right now, that your spirit man would rise up—that your soul would be at peace and in alignment with your spirit—who you are in Christ. I pray away any mindset that would seek to block you from receiving this teaching today; and for those of you who desperately need or want peace, that it overwhelms you right now. In Jesus's name. Amen.*

Chapter 1: Community Crime is a Result of Individual State of Being

I've been praying over the multitude of shootings that have arisen in our nation. After the most recent shooting—the Christian elementary school in Nashville, I asked God to show me what I can give to the community to help people understand what is happening.

I want to go over something with you that has drastically opened my eyes to the way I communicate with God, my husband, and my parents, and how I love—whether I am gentle and kind or not to those in our community. This is something that every person needs to know. Everything written in this chapter will change your life.

When anything goes against our natural hormones and God-given instincts, and more and more people become involved and committed to these things, we will see crime increase. The reason for this is because we have to literally harden our hearts against our God-given emotional instincts and state of homeostasis. One example of something society tends to embrace as "normal" is abortion. For someone to have an abortion, even if the mother and father believe at the time that it is the best route (though we know this to be a lie they are believing), they have to completely shut down their natural motherly and fatherly instincts to protect the baby. According to Focus on the Family, most women do not seek counseling or help until five years post abortion. Some never seek it. Some commit suicide. For those years following the abortion, until she is healed and delivered, a woman has a higher risk of making other

The Pathway to Transcendent Peace

types of decisions that will have a negative effect because they have had to shut off their emotions to be able to go through with it. You have to harden your heart against what nature tells you to do and what we were born and created for.

This is not to pick on anyone that's had an abortion or is considering an abortion as an option right now. This is simply to give one example of an act that hardens our heart as a society and leads to higher crime rates. I have worked with women and families who have had abortions or considered them. I've done this for about five years now, on a regular basis, and I would absolutely love to help you through this if it's something you would like to further discuss.

What we're seeing in our society now is a hardness of heart and a loss of compassion. When those are absent, and the symptoms are intensified, the crimes that are committed keep getting worse. Consider the recent Tennessee shooting where seven people lost their lives—those innocent children, teachers, janitor, and administrator—that is just cruelty.

Let's say the person was shamed at that school for thinking differently. Shame is *never* something we should put on someone. If they don't claim to be followers of Christ, it's not our job to shame or judge them at all. If they *are* followers of Christ, we are to confront them in *love*. There should be no shame involved. It must begin at the lower levels; if you want to change what's going on in society, you have to change yourself first.

It's interesting how many people come to me and want to be involved in praying for expelling Jezebel in our nation but don't want to get down and dirty and expose Jezebel in their own life. We all have tendencies that cause us to act in "Jezebellic" ways. It is part of the fallen nature. It's a consequence of being human.

So often, people discuss and pray, determined to lessen the crimes in our society. Sometimes, making a change in society may seem daunting. However, today I share this good news with you: we can change the world one life at a time by changing ourselves. It begins with healing at the bottom—individuals—and moves upward, toward the most

Chapter 1: Community Crime is a Result of Individual State of Being

influential parts of our world. We can *be* the solution and we can *share* the solution with those around us, bringing light and healing everywhere we go. This was and still is our command: to go and take ground for our great God. Together, we CAN and we WILL change the statistics of the crime happening around us. The information in this chapter paints a picture of how our individual health relates to community health, and how we can become aware and in control of how we consistently behave and respond to things that come our way.

We've all had moments when we were disconnected from people. There are things that happened in our lives that caused our heart to harden. This causes our connection circuits to be switched off. Hardness of heart does not mean that we are no longer affected by the situations that caused us to harden our hearts; it's actually quite the opposite. It (whatever the situation is or was for each of us) affected us so much that we are no longer able to operate in a humane way. Hardness of heart means that our soul—our mind, will, and emotions—is hard. That means there's no gentleness, there's no compassion, there's no love in the area in which we have become disconnected. When we try to stuff it and push it away, that causes us to have hardness of heart, and our hope is deferred. Hope deferred, in my opinion, is actually a mental and emotional disease, meaning, you don't believe in an area in which you once had faith. Problems arise when we harden our souls to something. We all do it. We all have done it. We do it as a means of protecting ourselves from experiencing pain again in the future. However, this is not healthy. We read in Proverbs that hope deferred makes the heart sick. It doesn't say, "might make" or "could make."

> Hope deferred makes the heart sick.
> (Proverbs 13:12, NIV)

Brené Brown is a big hero of mine. She is a social work researcher. In her very important and in-depth studies, she discovered that there is absolutely no such thing as hardening just one area of your heart. When we begin to harden our heart at all, we begin to numb our emotions. Unfortunately, we cannot selectively numb emotions. We cannot numb negative emotions such as pain, grief, and sadness, and still hope to

The Pathway to Transcendent Peace

feel joy, peace, and gladness. When we numb our emotions, we numb them all. We are created to be wholehearted people, so when we become hard-hearted, the hardness will slowly begin to take over every part of our lives. If it is left unchecked and unhealed, we will begin to live a life of pain that can cause depression and even suicidal and sociopathic behaviors.

We simply become who we know we do not want to be, which can cause us to negatively impact others and live in regret. But, what if we take the time to allow God to heal our deeply rooted wounds? What if we all (the body of Christ) allow ourselves to fully receive the healing God has for us, so that, though we have been hurt, we don't let hard-heartedness affect our lives any longer than it already has? What would happen to our society if we took all of our cares and burdens to the Lord and showed others how to do that too? You know as well as I do that our world would quickly become a different place. We would be healed people helping hurting people everywhere we go. We would ignite and fuel a true love revolution, and then maybe, just maybe, the world wouldn't have to turn to other sources for love; they would go directly to Jesus.

Once your heart is hardened, it is hard to have compassion in other areas. Brené Brown teaches from a social work standpoint that, socially, we cannot have negative emotions and feel-good emotions also. When we numb the bad things that happen to us, and our heart is hard toward them, we can't experience joy, love, and creativity; nor can we launch forward into becoming who we're called to be because a solid platform isn't there. We have essentially blocked our heart from feeling these things.

For example, if you are struggling with depression, you cannot accept and be fully in depression and still live in a place of wholeheartedness and the authenticity of truly being who God created you to be. You can't numb negative emotions that you are exhibiting—because of disappointment or hope deferred—and still experience joy to the fullest.

When we allow something to harden our heart, make hope deferred, or decide to not work through those things and take the time to go through the process to be healed, it is going to affect *generations*. I

Chapter 1: Community Crime is a Result of Individual State of Being

think that sometimes we think, "This is just what's happened to me; I don't understand it, so I'm just going to leave it there and move on." There's a difference between not understanding and fully submitting it to God versus having hope deferred because of what didn't happen that you expected to happen.

Christ can become our strength when we are weak. We can overcome any of these things, but as a life coach and pastor, I cannot help you if you're not going to be honest. You can only be as healed as you are honest.

If you live in a state of hope deferred or are hard-hearted in any area of your life, there's hope for you! I was humbled when God showed me all of the things above. God has been showing me my childhood lately in a new light. I'm having moments when I realize *this is why I'm this way*. I've been giving myself a lot of grace since God gave me this revelation, and I'm changing my actions because of it. Will you join me in this work to become healthy in order to positively *a*ffect future *generations?*

Causes of disconnection

When hope deferred or hard-heartedness operates in any area of our life, these areas are like targets on our chests, and we are easily triggered. At first, the hardness doesn't always manifest as something we show all the time, but we discover the sore area when we are hit. What is something that triggers you and makes you feel like you are disconnected from someone? We all have common triggers that push us into fight mode. The following are examples of what triggers me and causes me to go from a healthy emotional state to crossing my threshold and acting out of survival mode.

Let me paint you a picture: you are in the car, busy with your kids; it's loud, and you are tired because you worked all day. It's raining and windy outside, and you're trying to pay attention to the road. Your significant other wants to tell you a bunch of stories, and your children won't stop bantering about the same thing—all you're trying to do is pay attention to the road, get everyone home safely, get ready for bed, and just have one minute to yourself. These are triggers of mine that I'm describing now. In this moment, I am about to not be the loving mom I desire to be, and I'm about to explode. I need everyone to stop right now. I need the noise to decrease, and I need a minute.

I don't get that minute because they're kids. They don't understand, and that's not their fault. The problem is my lack of ability to emotionally regulate myself. I have a choice in these moments to snap, yell at them, and blame others for my emotional state of being at the time.

We all have expectations. Whenever I have expectations, and they aren't met, even though they were expected, and there was no communication that the expectations were changing, it can send me into a tailspin where I want to disconnect because things were not done in the way we discussed.

Things that trigger me into disconnecting from people:

- When my decisions are overruled with no explanation
- When I make a request and the opposite is done as if I wasn't heard
- When I feel disapproval
- When I'm confronted in a way that is not loving
- When I've asked someone to stop doing something and they continue to do it
- When I'm not able to finish my goals and check things off my list
- Constant messes (laundry piling up, dirty dishes, trash not taken out, etc.)
- Overwhelm from back pain or smells
- When I'm not feeling well and still have to live up to my daily expectations with no time to rest
- When I don't eat well
- When I don't drink enough water

Chapter 1: Community Crime is a Result of Individual State of Being

- When I don't have time for a hobby or outlet, or to be creative

If I don't have an outlet, something will probably trigger me if I don't make my voice heard. I want to be open and honest with you because I want you to make a list as well of what turns you off relationally. What flips your switch from being relational, humane, and understanding of people's needs, to being emotionally turned off, disconnected, and isolated?

We were not meant to disconnect. In the social and physiological world, we call it disconnection; but when we disconnect from those we love the most, we also disconnect from God. One way to tell that you're disconnected from people is if you cannot see, feel, or hear another's needs.

For example, our dog Abraham recently ended up having loose stools. I was not taking care of the dogs at that time; I was working, so Robyn was taking care of the dogs. This happened, and he said that Abraham looked at him very sadly because his stomach hurt. He snuggled into Robyn, and Robyn prayed over him. Abe wagged his tail like he was thankful for that moment of being embraced and comforted. Robyn put him outside, cleaned up the mess, and that was it; whereas, if Abraham had this happen on a day that Robyn's trigger threshold had been surpassed, he could have been quick to get frustrated that he had to clean up a mess, and he may have mumbled and complained and yelled at Abe. In that moment, he chose to *connect*.

In that moment, if Robyn had thought *Why again? Why me? I'm too busy, I don't have time*, he could have flipped from caring and serving to *it being all about him*. We've all been there; when we're in the moment, we can completely forget that we could embrace someone, pray for them, and have compassion for what they're going through. We cannot do these things if we are hard-hearted and disconnected from society; this has caused us to become a very selfish people.

In the past, church people have told me, "You have the spirit of isolation on you." I never understood that because I'm super friendly, I love people, and I've always had a life-of-the-party personality. I didn't understand what that meant because I wasn't alone; I was with a lot

The Pathway to Transcendent Peace

of people. But behind the scenes, I struggled with severe depression. I could be in a room where I'm the center of attention but still feel alone. I didn't have the language for it at the time, nor did I even recognize it was happening.

You can be with your spouse and still feel isolated. You may have chosen to put yourself there by allowing yourself to become disconnected because you had an expectation that wasn't met, or because of whatever triggered you. It's not that we're a victim; it's that we didn't know—or we chose not—to become emotionally aware enough to step back for a moment and take a break.

Robyn and I are very good about telling each other when we need ten minutes to ourselves. One of us takes our break to get recharged and comes back just fine, while the other one steps up and becomes the better half at that moment. I recommend having a "trigger word" for when you know you're reaching your threshold and are about to cross it. It's important to communicate with the person you are closest to, that you're about to get beyond frustrated. However, I don't recommend telling someone that they are being triggered. When we flip into that frame of disconnection, it's super frustrating, especially as Christians, because of our beliefs, morals, and values—who we are. We want to reflect that to our children, but we're still human.

> But he said to me, "My grace is sufficient for you, for my power is made perfect in weakness." Therefore I will boast all the more gladly about my weaknesses, so that Christ's power may rest on me. (2 Corinthians 12:9)

I'm telling you what I told Robyn, and even my four-year-old: my triggers. These are the things I want you to know that I try to avoid. When these things happen, we need a break to breathe and come back down and realize that whoever we're dealing with is a person with emotions. It may be your coworkers, your boss, your children, your spouse—it could be anyone.

I believe this will shed some light for people who struggle with anger. The Bible says to *be angry and sin not*. God knows that we have

Chapter 1: Community Crime is a Result of Individual State of Being

emotions and we become frustrated, but there is a moment when we choose how we will act. Making a choice in the moment to set a boundary for yourself and make it known—a mental break or whatever the boundary may be—is what will truly change how you deal with anger and other adverse emotions. The Holy Spirit will rule in our heart and guide our mind in Christ Jesus if we will let Him.

> Let the peace of Christ rule in your hearts; since as members of one body you were called to peace. And be thankful. (Colossians 3:15)

In that verse, the root word for "rule" means "referee." Anytime we're out of bounds, we give the Holy Spirit and other people permission to blow the whistle to tell us we're out of bounds.

We want to reflect our true character and values, so we need to do whatever is necessary to bring us back to reality for a moment and realize these are humans. We don't want to destroy their hearts, lives, or minds, and make them critical. We can ask God to help us and be our strength in times of weakness. One question I like to ask myself is *how can I best reflect my character and values in this moment?*

This is the time to make the decision; if we switch into a mode of disconnection, we also turn off our connection with God. When we're disconnected, we don't want to hear what anyone has to say; we just want to fight. Anything anyone has to say becomes a reason to fight or shut down and go hide in a corner. It depends on how you as an individual deal with things.

What can we do to come back into that place of connection once we're disconnected?

We can simply make a *choice*. We have to lay down what's frustrating us. We need to become better at communicating and setting boundaries; and we need to practice being mindful and aware of what's going on around us. This is also the key to a peaceful marriage.

When we go into that hardness of heart mode:

The Pathway to Transcendent Peace

- We get disgusted with things that are going on
- We can go into victim mode
- We can start commanding people to do things to make us happy
- We care only for ourselves at the moment
- We become critical of everything around us
- We can go into attack mode
- We can go into a brewing mode where we're acting nice but we're not actually connecting with the other person

Then it can turn *inward*. If you don't communicate your needs and set healthy boundaries, self-hatred, self-critical talk, extreme depression, and suicidal thoughts can come in.

I was suicidal on and off many times from my teenage years until I was about twenty-four years old. I didn't have the knowledge then that I'm sharing with you now. I didn't have the language to say that I was feeling disconnected because someone made me feel not wanted or not approved; I'd disconnect and not care what anyone had to say.

The truth is that we never *not care*. We show how much we do care by disconnecting from the entire humanity of our being—our compassion, our ability to feel love, joy, hope, peace, etc. By making it such a big deal, we decide not to feel those things at all. Having the words to understand what's happening in us, and compassion for ourselves, helps us have compassion for other people.

Isolation

If we stay isolated, our heart can become sick because it's also the hope deferred of getting back into conversing with our spouse or connecting relationally with whoever it is we're disconnected from. This can lead to the death of others spiritually as well. If God told us to give someone a word, and we're hard-hearted toward them, but that word was going to change their life and we chose not to do it, that's a pretty big deal. If you're hard-hearted toward everyone at the moment, and the Holy Spirit is trying to referee but you choose not to listen to Him,

Chapter 1: Community Crime is a Result of Individual State of Being

you're disobeying God. That can lead to death in your own spiritual life. I'm not saying just one time; God has a lot of grace, but if it becomes a pattern, over time it can lead to death. All of our decisions have consequences, so let's be emotionally responsible and recognize that.

> The LORD is close to the brokenhearted and saves those who are crushed in spirit. (Psalm 34:18, NIV)

This is very important to remember because we are crushed in that moment. That's why we go into a mode of isolation and disconnection. I told you all of my triggers, but I'm okay because I boast in those things. In my weakness, God is my strength. I look forward to God showing up as my strength.

> Turn to me and be gracious to me, for I am lonely and afflicted. Relieve the troubles of my heart and free me from my anguish. (Psalm 25:16-17, NIV)

The writer of this psalm gives us a prayer that we can pray to God in times of loneliness; disconnection ushers in loneliness. These are things you can write down to pray whenever you're in this moment of loneliness. It's not weak to say, "I feel lonely and disconnected from you right now." I think it's very healthy to say that, even if it's hard.

When Robyn and I were first married, I did not talk about my emotions. If I wanted you to know my emotions, I would show you them and make them clear. Otherwise, I'd keep them to myself. It wasn't something that was a public matter to me. I was always taught to shut up and deal with things myself. My way of doing that was through writing.

Robyn came to me in our first month or two of marriage, sat next to me on our bed, and told me everything I felt. I said, "I didn't give you permission to talk about my emotions. I didn't want to." I was very hurt in the moment.

He said that God showed him. I said, "Well, I didn't give God permission to tell you my emotions."

Robyn said, "Well, He did, so it's for a purpose."

The Pathway to Transcendent Peace

That actually helped my hardened heart. I learned that I could trust someone with my emotions. I thought emotions were things people ran over. I'm a life coach now, so it's natural that I deal a lot with emotions. As believers and ministers, we have to have healthy emotions to help other people; and really, to enjoy everyday life ourselves. The Enemy would love to keep you stuck and feeling lonely.

Effects of isolation:

- Makes a person or a family vulnerable to Satan's attack
- Can cause a person to make improper decisions based on fleshly motives
- Isolation from the church opens up the mind for influence from the world, flesh, and the devil
- Causes disconnection between people and prevents accountability. In marriage counseling, this is often where we see porn addiction, cheating, believing lies [their spouse is cheating when they are not, their spouse does not find them attractive or smart, etc. If suicidal, believing the lie that the world would be better off without them or that they are a burden]
- Intensifies the burdens of life
- Loneliness
- Can lead to depression
- Can cause a person or family to have a negative attitude toward the church, their spouse, or anyone else; or go into "enemy mode" and feel like their spouse, kids, or others close to them are their enemy, rather than their friend. In reality, it's because they haven't had the teaching and understanding to implement being thoughtful and setting healthy boundaries.
- Inhibits ministry

We all know someone who has a victim mindset. It makes everything feel big. One small thing that happens can put you over your trigger because you're in survival mode.

Chapter 1: Community Crime is a Result of Individual State of Being

Did we get to this place of isolating ourselves because we were bullied as kids? I never thought about that because I feel like "bully" is a trigger word; it's very hot right now, and it's overused because the victim mentality is also overused. In the same sense, people want to feel accepted and validated. It's important that we take a moment to ask ourselves *Am I critical of myself because my parents flipped into enemy mode and were not in relationship mode where they could recognize the needs of other people?* They didn't have the skills that we're now learning in this generation to be able to deal with the things that challenged them. Were we bullied because when our parents flipped into this, they seemed like a predator and didn't know how to turn it off? Maybe it wasn't your parents; it could have been anyone.

Forgive them. Forgive yourself. Remember to ask yourself when you're about to be flipped over your threshold, *How do I reflect my true character and values in this conversation? How do I self-soothe in overwhelming circumstances?* These are things to think about before you get into those circumstances, and then have them already written down or speak them over yourself. We also made *Soaking in Scripture* videos that you can play. Tell yourself: *I am in charge of my emotions and how I respond. I will not allow my flesh to respond negatively; I will stay in charge and in control. God will be my strength in weakness.*

Joy

Joy has a different definition than you may think. From a social work perspective, joy is the ability to be connected at all times to someone who fully accepts you for who you are. It's a state of being. We cannot actually feel that connectedness and joy apart from God. It is something that doesn't exist because who's going to accept us perfectly and wholeheartedly for everything we do? As much as I love Robyn, I don't think I can love him like Christ loves him. Christ's love is extravagant, and I'm still learning to experience that on a daily basis.

The one Person we can feel true joy with is God. The moment we shut down the connection with Him, we will have a decrease of dopamine and the feel-good hormones and chemicals that are released into our brain. A lack of dopamine and serotonin leads to a lack of sleep. It

The Pathway to Transcendent Peace

can lead to ADHD, depression, Alzheimer's, and a whole list of other things, because we're chemically imbalanced when we're not in relationship with God.

God wants us to be in relationship with Him because He loves us, but it's also a benefit to our health to not get jaded or hard-hearted. Hope deferred makes the heart sick. I keep getting more and more revelation about how losing our hope, joy, and peace can make us sick in many ways. It benefits us to learn how to live in a constant state of joy. When we do, it takes courage to live there.

I had to really work through the fear of being let down and disappointed. I felt like if I trusted again, I was going to be let down, and then I wasn't going to be in a place of joy anymore. I didn't know how to respond when I was let down. We can ask God how to respond when we're let down. We don't have to shut down; we can turn to our spouse or to God when we feel let down, and seek relationship.

When we get out of the place of connection with people, we show what we call our "true colors." It is actually the opposite of that. Satan would want you to believe you are what you do, but we know that is not true. We need to stop and recognize our triggers and when they're about to happen. When we know they're about to happen, we need to take a moment, take a breath, and intentionally take three to five minutes to do whatever is necessary to get back into that place of peace. We can say, "Holy Spirit, anchor me down; rule and reign in my heart. Guard my mind in Christ Jesus."

We can pray, *Holy Spirit, come help me reflect on You in this situation. Help who I really am and what I really value come out of me at this time, even though it's not what I feel like doing. Thank You that I can rely on You to shine in my weakness. I give You permission to speak through me now. You are that peace that rules in my atmosphere, in Jesus's name.*

I recently told Robyn that one of the most recent dogs we rescued is reactive but not aggressive. I never thought about it this way until tonight, but if I was a dog, I would probably behave the same way on some days. I would react to something, but I'm not truly an aggressive

Chapter 1: Community Crime is a Result of Individual State of Being

person. It's just because I didn't recognize my triggers in time to not switch into enemy mode. I didn't really want to bite anyone—I wasn't truly aggressive—I just flipped into that mode because that's what life told me to do. Humans can be reactive and not aggressive. Just because we act a certain way doesn't mean our intention is to hurt someone. When we encounter something that sends us into survival mode, we may snap because we can't hear anything going on around us and we fear for our survival. It is still destructive and is caused by a trigger that puts us over our threshold.

Interestingly, whoever is closest to an aggressive dog will be the victim if the dog is past its threshold. When this happens, they don't see anything around them; they go for whatever is the closest thing to them. It's nothing personal; it's just how it is. If we apply this to ourselves, it is easy to see that we don't reason in the moments we are in survival mode. Our thinking is decreased, and it is hard to pull up words that we want. All reasoning and problem solving gets pushed to the back because your body has used your nervous system to go into freeze, fight, or flight response. This means that blood is shunted from your brain into organs of your body that need it the most. When that happens, we are scientifically unable to process things in our mind. That's why, whenever we're in enemy mode with whoever we're closest to, the one who is in the line of fire is the one that gets hit. They're not necessarily the one that did anything wrong.

I address this behavior with the dogs by helping them snap out of survival mode and into a different command they're already confident in. Then I help them get out extra energy based on the energy they're feeling. I give them an outlet for that. I give them something to do that's safe, healthy, and restores their health. For you, that could be working out, going for a walk, biking, sitting with your dogs, etc.

I can train dogs and get their aggression under control, and I think we can do the same with humans. It's a matter of understanding behavior. Ask God what the long-term effects of not connecting with people are. I told you some of them: the lack of dopamine and serotonin—our feel-good hormones and the chemicals in our brain that get released throughout our body. Those affect our neurological system—our heart

The Pathway to Transcendent Peace

rate, respiratory rates, blood pressure—things like that. If you're struggling with anger, you will eventually struggle with high blood pressure, a high heart rate, and other things that keep you out of that place of peace. The world calls it anxiety.

I want you to know there is hope! You can regain your control and composure by surrendering your weakness to the Holy Spirit and letting Him be made strong in you. We will discuss more behaviors in the following chapters that can steal our peace on a daily basis, and how to repair the built-in peace system God created us with.

I bless you, and I bless your relationships. I bless your neurological system to be in perfect operating order as God created it to be. I declare you will live in joy with God and with others. You will not be depressed; you will be wholeheartedly courageous, brave, and trust in God to not let you down. I speak to all hope deferred, and I send healing into your heart. I repent on behalf of God, saying I'm sorry for any time I've not met your expectations. I send the blood of Jesus into your heart and a healing river to flow through you to bring hope and life back again. I cancel the effects of self-hatred and criticism you've had toward yourself or that anyone else has had over you. We pray this in Jesus's name. Amen.

Chapter 2: Peace-Robbing Behaviors

There are behaviors that we exhibit—that we operate in—that are ungodly. These hold us back from being able to fully enter into peace and remain there. Some of us operate in them all of the time and don't know how to get out of those cycles; and the rest of us tend to fall back on them when we are in survival mode or going through a crisis. It's important that we open our heart to the Lord and give Him permission to highlight any area in which we occasionally or consistently struggle. I will also help you to understand what to do with these and how to let them go forever.

What do I mean by ungodly behaviors? Here are some to consider:

- Control
- Manipulation
- Taking matters into your own hands
- Worry
- Panic
- Fear of the unknown
- Fear of what is going on in our government
- Fear of disconnection with people because it is in our nature to connect
- Fear of rejection

The Pathway to Transcendent Peace

There are many unhealthy behaviors that we get into, and we tend to try to change who we are in order to compensate for being afraid of not being enough. You can immediately recognize how these could be weapons that Satan will use to steal the peace of God from you. I have good news; you can demand that he return sevenfold the peace he has stolen from you!

When we are fearful for our survival, fearful of our reputation being tarnished, or fearful of being rejected by someone we love and respect, we automatically go into survival mode. It's part of our primal being and how we have developed over the years.

That innate default to defend ourselves is good when it is used for survival, for a reasonable period of time, in order to get through a difficult or traumatic situation. If you're not sleeping at night, and you're in survival mode, you reprioritize things based on the crisis you're in and revert back into those mechanisms. But then you're stressed out; your cortisol levels are higher, which raises your blood sugar, affects your adrenals, and then affects how your nerve endings work. I'll give you an example from my life. Imagine having a medically needy baby and being up with him several times every night for over sixteen months, while trying to homeschool, run a ministry and two businesses, parent a toddler, be a good wife, be a faithful church member, etc. During the day, the stress of not sleeping made it harder to respond the way my spirit wanted, to things that normally wouldn't have been an issue had we not gone without adequate sleep for a year and a half. I'm sure you have your own story and that, on some level, you can relate!

We are created to thrive, not just survive

I live to help you live up to your fullest potential found in abundant life. My favorite verse is John 10:10:

> The thief comes only in order to steal and kill and destroy.
> I came that they may have and enjoy life, and have it in abundance [to the full, until it overflows].

Chapter 2: Peace-Robbing Behaviors

As you continue through this book, we're going to uncover things that prevent you from living this abundant life, and you can then learn to continually experience it!

Why do we go into survival mode and mechanisms? We talked about fear, rejection, and other root issues, but there are behaviors that we use when we haven't developed any other options for overcoming difficult and vulnerable situations. Discovering and overturning these behaviors will require honesty.

This will take *discipline*. We need to develop other options for dealing with vulnerability, fear, distress, etc. When our wellbeing is at risk, we go into distress. What you don't know is that this is the definition of codependency. As a life coach, I have many clients and friends to whom I have mentioned that it would be really helpful if we could go through some codependency material together, and they *run*. They think it's crazy. They think I've diagnosed them with a problem and that I've assessed it incorrectly, but that is the definition of codependency. It is when we have developed unhealthy ways of operating in our relationships due to being in survival mode—instead of thriving mode—in those relationships. This births codependent behavior. It is my heart's desire for you to be able to recognize these behaviors and get free from them so you can be in a place of shalom and wholeness!

Continually operating in these survival behaviors poses a problem. Survival mode was put inside of us to go into when we are in danger, but when we are never taught how to get out of it and into contentment—how to flip out of it into peace—that is when codependency happens. Habitual tendencies create the label of codependency, not one-time survival mechanisms.

I do not believe that once you are codependent, you are codependent forever. I am thriving and successful, and I was once super codependent. Now I am very satisfied and fulfilled in my relationships. I manage things really well; I can bless people, I can love them and not hold onto them—and I never try to control anyone. I can watch people come and go from my life and not take it personally, and I can still love deeply without restraint, even with the vulnerability of knowing it might never be reciprocated. Let's look at some causes of codependent tendencies.

Abandonment issues

If you've ever had a trust issue from something that happened in your life—at any point in your life—you've learned some (typically unhealthy) behaviors for coping with your trust being broken, with abuse, or with abandonment. Abuse feels like abandonment plus *so much more*. It is a form of abandonment because your abuser abandoned your trust; they abandoned who you thought they were, and turned into an abusive individual.

You probably don't engage in meaningful conversation that makes you feel okay being vulnerable and talking to someone about these things—talking to me, our team, your pastors, or whoever is in your sphere of influence—so you can get set free! This is not something you do instead of talking to God; it is imperative you talk to Him. As you do, He will likely also direct you to someone He has anointed to help you through the healing process.

The truth sets us free! It's okay to admit, "I was controlling in this situation." When you say that, you acknowledge it; but it's what you do about it that matters. I'm going to give you strategies to overcome that. For example, we have a course in our life-coaching program called *Crisis Coaching*. In crisis coaching, one of the goals is to help you walk through whatever difficult situation you may be facing, from a healed perspective, even though you may be up against trauma. That way, you can come out of it, and you can shift back into your new normal without being in that crisis mode and crisis mindset—or survival mode, mechanisms, behaviors, tendencies, fill in the blank.

Our goal is to help you heal so that when you experience another crisis that's similar, you will not overreact. You can just remember what you did in this crisis situation that worked really well, and practice those same behaviors if faced with a similar situation in the future.

Crisis coaching is super important! I just love walking beside you and being with you amidst what you're going through. We are never

Chapter 2: Peace-Robbing Behaviors

alone, but I think that sometimes, as the body of Christ, we don't have time (or we don't make time) to connect with people like we should. Even if you're not facing a traumatic crisis right now, at some point, you most likely have! So, let's take a look at the types of trauma that are out there.

A good resource is *Joy Stream* teachings and materials by *Life Model Works*. If you read this, you will learn that there are two types of trauma: Type A trauma and Type B trauma.

- Type A Trauma: blunt trauma; direct force; direct abuse
- Type B Trauma: indirect trauma; abandonment—not having your emotional needs met

If you have experienced either of these types of trauma (we all have at some point, if we're being honest), you still come out with similar issues as those who have Type A trauma, which stems from direct abuse. Some people are bewildered because they can't figure out why certain types of people gravitate toward them—people who are needy, need rescuers, are victims, don't understand how to have healthy relationships—or why they attract people who are abusive. Typically, it's because they haven't found that place of peace yet. When they do, they will be able to meet the needs of other people in healthy ways that are rewarding and beautiful. That sets them free to live up to their fullest potential because their needs will be met. You can teach them to get their particular need met if you're in that position of authority in their lives.

If you don't know how to do that, emotionally unhealthy people are going to keep coming to you and replaying that same cycle in which they are unknowingly bound. Once you meet that need, it calms them down and you can even cast out demons.

There is more than one way to cast out a demon. When I meet someone's need, if that need and that void was the reason the demon had the ability to stay there, what's it going to do now? It's *not* going to be able to stay. It's going to try to come back the next time the person's need arises, so we have to teach them how to get it met in godly ways. This is going from surviving to thriving.

The Pathway to Transcendent Peace

So what does it look like when we have experienced trauma, and the effects of it are still lingering in our lives? Here are a few practical examples of how trauma might manifest.

When we're mad that we can't stick to our routine

I am super busy, as you just read. I run a ministry, a life-coaching business, and a dog-training business. Over the past couple of months, I've started to get help for this, which is a big relief. I am beyond thankful, and of course, my husband, Robyn, does a great job. We also have two small kids, and I have a stepson—my bonus son.

Joseph, our ten-month-old, has continual feeding therapy and doctor appointments. I have to do his therapy three times a day at home, in addition to his appointments, feeding-tube maintenance, etc. I try to juggle these and be a good wife, mother, minister, lover of people, have integrity, answer emails, etc., so it's very important that I stay on schedule. I have so many responsibilities and I don't want to miss any of them. And, more importantly, I don't want to mess any of them up!

I'll give you an example. Tonight, twenty minutes after we put our three-year-old, Asher, to bed, I started to record a teaching. Asher decided that he needed to get up to use the restroom—and the baby woke up for milk thirty minutes after we got him down for the night. After we finally got the kids settled and the dogs pottied, loved, played with, trained, and in bed, I finally sat down to work; but soon, everyone was awake again! I just wanted to cry because I still had so much work to do!

What I've learned is that my job is to meet the needs of my family first. So if I have to stop what I'm doing—work, ministry, whatever—it's okay. I have had to practice that. Even though my schedule is important, and I want to get these things done well, my priority is my family. Some nights, I'm just not able to get done what I intend. An hour and a half past when I was supposed to start working, I was exhausted, and my work did not get done to my satisfaction because I was so tired.

Chapter 2: Peace-Robbing Behaviors

I have learned that it's an opportunity to show my children that they're not an inconvenience. It's an opportunity for me to show Jesus that I will allow Him to change my plans whenever He wants.

So if you get frustrated when your routine gets changed, when what you planned for the day changes, or your schedule gets changed, that is a sign that you're suffering from the lingering effects of trauma. You will begin to recognize when you're operating in these behaviors.

Making false accusations because of a habitual critical mindset

It is very hurtful to be accused of something we did not do, but when we are caught up in this cycle, that is what we do to others. Some examples of this may be:

- Accusing someone of doing something they haven't actually done, but you've programmed yourself to operate in a critical mindset
- A video pops up on your significant other's phone and it's just an ad from a game they are playing; you didn't know what it was, but you thought they were watching something inappropriate when they weren't, and you accuse them
- Someone walks by and your significant other looks in that direction; they're not looking at the person in an inappropriate way, but you accuse them of doing so anyway

Being critical of other people comes from our survival mechanisms. We get nitpicky when we're in survival mode.

Let me give you a real-life example. I worked in the pulmonary sepsis ICU for a long time as a registered nurse. When a patient is coding, or their heart stops, or it's in a rhythm that is not functional, like an atrial flutter or something, or obviously A Fib, there is a level of nitpicking that is necessary to save that person's life.

- Make sure this drip is running at this rate and at this dose for a person that weighs this much.

The Pathway to Transcendent Peace

- Make sure *this* person is in charge of *this*
- Have the chaplain with the family
- Push *this* medicine at *this* time
- Write it down so you don't forget it

You're running all of these nitpicky but very important details in the midst of a crisis. As nurses, we live in crisis mode for so long because we respond to back-to-back crisis situations all day, every shift. That's just the nature of the job. It's literally life or death. I'm sharing a dramatic example, but this was my everyday life. It wasn't dramatic for me. Even if you're not an ICU RN, going from crisis to crisis makes us fearful that we're going to miss a detail that can harm someone. That transferred to my everyday life, and I became critical—critical that I was making major mistakes, blaming myself and others, and keeping myself accountable for unrealistic expectations that were unnecessary—but I didn't see that. No one had ever taught me how to shift out of my normal into the real world. I didn't even realize I needed to do that! It can almost begin to take on forms of post-traumatic stress disorder (PTSD).

I was used to everything being life or death and depending on me in every scenario. Flashback to nursing—if you don't do something right, you get your license taken away. It hurts the family, it hurts the patient, and you don't want to do that. The whole reason you're there is to love people and help them. That's why you went through all the heck of school to do it!

When you're in something like that, or absolutely any scenario that puts you in survival mode, you have to be able to switch out of it. I never did that. I never really embraced the new normal—not when I lived and worked every day with life-or-death situations. It is not a life-or-death situation if the puzzle doesn't get picked up!

Incidentally, that's why a lot of nurses don't last in the ICU more than two or three years—because of PTSD, the survival mechanism routine that you get into, the high blood sugar, your cortisol levels being high all the time—those types of things. It could also be why some people move from job to job; they have not been taught how to cope with stressors, or change them, and feel like they have to escape.

Chapter 2: Peace-Robbing Behaviors

Let's take it one step further. Let's say you're reading this, and you just wished you could escape your home or work scenario; maybe even a friendship. Maybe you committed to something, and you don't know how you can keep on surviving. I can guarantee that you are critical of yourself because you can't rely on others. Then you feel you're just as responsible and you can't rely on yourself. There is hope, and there is a way out of these things without having to leave the scene. Don't get me wrong; there are times when it is necessary to leave, but sometimes you can't. Sometimes you're not supposed to leave. For example, a child that is not happy at home cannot leave because he or she isn't old enough.

I am here to teach you how to overcome these things so you can get your needs met in Christ and thrive in the environment you're in. You can REMAIN in His peace without being moved by the words or actions of those around you. This is the peace of Christ that goes above and beyond our understanding. This is HIS desire for you, and because of that, He wouldn't withhold it from you. In fact, He's TRYING to GET it to you!

When we're critical, it's actually for our protection because:

- We're afraid we're not doing something good enough
- We're afraid we're going to harm someone if it isn't done right
- We're doing it as a defense mechanism. We're criticizing someone for something we should be doing. We subconsciously want to make them feel bad about it so we don't look bad and our wellbeing isn't at risk.
- We're afraid of letting others down—people pleasing

We're in survival mode when we don't embrace the process

Let's say you wanted to start a company, and you gave up after six months because you had the vision of having A-Z completed in five months. The sixth month is here, and you're still working on laying the foundation. You're upset; you feel like you failed, and you give up.

That birthing phase, and laying the foundation, is honestly when a lot of people stop. The reason could be financial, emotional, or just frustration, and you're blaming yourself and being critical of yourself. Anything good takes time—a long time!

Don't get me wrong; I believe in goals and all of those types of expectations, but if something doesn't happen in my timeframe, as long as I'm striving toward those goals, it's perfectly okay with me. We're only called to do what we're called to do right now, with the resources we've been given now.

If you have something the Lord has called you to do, He'll provide the resources for you at the appropriate time. But what do we do while we're waiting on those? We must make use of the resources that God has given us right now—we embrace those and make the most of them, and we *enjoy* it! We don't complain that we're not where we want to be. This is another form of being critical and not allowing the grace of God to cover us and then give it to others. It is also a key sign that we have not been nurtured well in our lives, therefore, we do not know how to nurture what we're building in the process. We will dig deeper into this in the nurturing chapter.

Joyce Meyer said, "I may not be where I want to be, but thank God I'm not where I used to be." I couldn't find this to be more true! May we all stop right now and apologize to ourselves, and to God, for not giving grace to ourselves and those around us. God understands why we haven't, but He also understands how to help us grow in grace—He is more than willing to help us do that!

Healing is often a process

Another sign that we don't embrace the process well is praying for healing for someone and not understanding why the healing didn't manifest right then. Now, we want to be balanced. Of course we want to pray for that healing to manifest immediately. We want to believe for it, and we want to pursue it; but sometimes, healing is a process. Just because we haven't seen it doesn't mean it hasn't happened.

Chapter 2: Peace-Robbing Behaviors

When we can't pray and make it appear, we feel as though we failed and/or God has failed us. Sometimes God wants to walk us through the process of healing because He's more concerned with our heart, our character, and our relationship with Him, than He is with an instantaneous result. Not being okay and not being comfortable with that waiting period is where we often go wrong as sent ones.

In the Bible, the word "wait" means to expectantly look for something. It's not a passive term. It's not a noun; it's a verb. A verb is something with action, so we are expectantly waiting on the Lord. Just because I'm expectantly waiting doesn't mean I have any less faith than someone who just saw the miracle manifest. Actually, we might have more!

Another way lingering trauma manifests is a tendency to get snippy with people when we have to repeat ourselves. A known trait that I have had to overcome and continually work on is being patient when I explain something but people don't understand it the first or second time. Instead of getting frustrated and feeling like I am not able to be heard, I have learned to step back and ask *what could I be teaching in a better way*? What is something that I can work on in myself to improve how what I'm trying to say comes across?

Billie Boatright was one of my previous mentors; I have heard her and Andy Andrews both teach that the quality of answer you receive from those listening to you depends on the quality of the question you ask.

It's really important that we be *intentional* with our language and that we make an effort to communicate with clarity, with purpose, and with life so we don't create death with our words and get an answer we're not wanting.

Sometimes we're in a hurry; we explain things in a hurry, and people need us to repeat what we said. Sometimes we *do* take the time to explain it all, and they still don't get it, or they just forgot, and you have to explain it again.

It is investing in your relationship, and it's also a spiritual discipline practice of self-control and self-regulation to stop and patiently repeat what you were saying the first time. If they asked you, there's a reason

The Pathway to Transcendent Peace

for why they forgot. Be patient with people who are asking you to repeat yourself. If you get snippy with people often, and it's not just a one-time issue because you didn't sleep well, this is indicative of codependent behavior.

When we have hope deferred or trauma from a non-loving encounter, these things can happen:

- We gradually slip into survival mode
- In our relationships, we act out of fear for our wellbeing—our sense of safety may be at risk
- We don't allow time to nurture the situation, or ourselves, through a process
- We are constantly on guard, defending ourselves and creating scenarios to defend ourselves before there is even a need

The Bible specifically tells us not to practice how we are going to argue with someone. We are not to preconceive arguments or how we're going to defend ourselves when someone comes against us or disagrees with us. Sometimes that feels like persecution, but it's not.

We are not to practice defending ourselves. If you are doing this, you either need to be healed from trauma or perhaps you're doing something you should not be doing. Those are the times we feel the need to defend ourselves.

I used the word "nurturing." We must nurture ourselves through the process. I struggled with these issues until I understood what nurturing was. Then I was able to get out of the cycle.

Chapter 3: How To Get Out of the Cycle

We learn to see ourselves and the world around us with eyes of trust and peace that come from being nurtured. I will tell you how to get to that viewpoint soon!

We see truth through the brokenness of trauma (Type A or Type B) that we have experienced in our lives. When we do that, we plant seeds of bitterness, anger, and brokenness. We just see pieces of a puzzle, when the Lord's desire is for us to see the whole picture from His perspective—with the mind of Christ.

We are to be Spirit-led, not soul-led. When we're broken, our soul is typically the part that leads us. *BUT* there is hope for you, and there is hope for me! You can give yourself grace and encouragement knowing that when the light of the Lord shines into your soul, and radiates from your soul, you can become healed and whole—a beautiful masterpiece once again.

We have to acknowledge our old behavior. The first step to getting over an issue is realizing that it's something we struggle with.

Recognizing when you're out of control

This is a big step that I like to talk about. At times, I have been unmanageable and out of control in certain areas. I'm sure that you have been too. That's nothing to be ashamed about; it's simply something to

The Pathway to Transcendent Peace

be aware of. And we must say and do what we can to make amends with those we love and those we hate. Honestly, we need to do what we can to make amends because the Lord said that He wishes for us to strive to live in peace with all.

Acknowledge that you're out of control; for example, being cut off on the road while you're driving and responding negatively. It literally doesn't change the other driver—it *never* will. So what is the point of getting upset and allowing your soul to be moved by an external stimulus that you have zero control over? Zero!

This was very freeing for me because now I can be around drug addicts; I can be around alcoholics; I can be around codependents; I can be around insecure people and not take their insecurity on as my own. Someone who is broken sees other people through broken lenses; meaning, I see your insecurity, and I know you're afraid that I'm gonna take your position. You're afraid that I'm prettier than you, or better than you, or I am more confident than you. So you start to avoid me; but I am going to seek you out to make sure that I build your confidence and you trust in yourself. That I honor you, respect you, and meet those needs that are not being met, that you feel insecure about in your life. This is what Jesus would do. He wouldn't lash out at someone because they are insecure. Because He is whole, He can see where they're broken and not take things personally. He can listen to them but still be in control of His emotions and responses. He wants to meet their needs so they become fulfilled in their lives with Him. May we all strive to do this with the most difficult people around us!

That's what you can do from a *whole perspective*, but a *broken perspective* says: it's about me. I did something wrong. What did I not do to please them? How can I make it right? And just like that, you start to take control of the situation.

When you're operating from a place of freedom and a place of peace, you literally can just love people because you love who you are, you love where you're at, and the light just shines out of you so brightly. You want them to be able to love in the place they are at too!

Chapter 3: How To Get Out of the Cycle

I'm going to explain to you a little bit of the visions that the Lord has been giving me with regard to this subject. It's been nearly two years now that I have been diligently seeking the Lord for emotional balance in my life. Of course I've always thought about it, but I've been very intentional for the last couple of years to study it. And man, has it made a difference in my life! I started practicing mindfulness and just being aware. What does mindfulness look like for me, and why is it so powerful?

I started taking three times a day, every day, to step back and intentionally ask:

- Am I responding out of love?
- What is the root that is causing me to be moved from my place of peace right now?
- Am I overexcited?
- Am I overdramatic?
- Am I fearful?
- Am I being defensive?
- Are my emotional circuits on or off right now?
- How am I responding?
- Am I aware of myself?
- Are my muscles tense?
- Where am I spiritually, mentally, physically, and emotionally?
- What is Jesus doing here right now?

Then I would go back into whatever chaos there was that I was ensuing at the time. I struggled because I was getting frustrated with myself for being moved out of a place of peace and mindfulness, and because I became overwhelmed when I would go back into a highly stressful environment.

Fast forward to a few months ago; I had three dreams, one after another, that kept me up all night. After I woke up from them, I had to find out what the Lord was saying to me! I asked, "Lord, please help me understand what you're trying to reveal to me!"

What the Lord revealed to me through that was that I didn't really receive the nurturing I needed when I was young. My parents intended to provide it, and they did the best they could, but they were never really nurtured either. They had high expectations, and emotions were just the last thing to really be acknowledged. That's because their parents didn't know how to do that either. So again, it's no one's fault is my point, but nurturing did not play a significant role in my childhood.

At twelve years old, I was told by my mom, "I've raised you; raise yourself." Then she said, "I am done doing what you need, and I am going to go do me." And she went away emotionally.

I didn't have a chance to experience my childhood. And I didn't have time to mourn it. I worked full time in a nursing home from the time I was nine years old until I turned eighteen. I was always very responsible. I worked full time, sixty to seventy hours a week. I didn't get paid. I was technically volunteering, but it was work for me. When I became of age, I ended up becoming the head nurse of that facility immediately after I graduated from high school.

I now understand because of those dreams the Lord gave me. Because He's so good, I finally had language to put with the issues I was experiencing in my everyday life. I didn't know how to overcome them because I didn't have language for them!

But when the Lord said, *"What you're missing is nurturing,"* I started being aware.

Robyn and I would hold each other accountable and say, "Oh, that wasn't a nurturing way to handle this situation. How can we help nurture each other in the midst of what we are going through now? How can I nurture my husband through what he's going through?" Honestly, this revelation has been completely life-changing for me.

I grew exponentially in my understanding of mindfulness and awareness. I practiced that with intention and asked myself, *Am I being*

Chapter 3: How To Get Out of the Cycle

nurturing toward myself? Am I being nurturing toward others? Just being aware of this fostered much growth.

Since I received that revelation, it's just like I spoke it; I forgave—I forgave myself. I told the Holy Spirit that I don't know what it looks like to overcome the need to be nurtured.

That was the other thing; in my life, I've experienced rejection from almost every woman leader that I've been with. I was very hard to love, so I somewhat understand their perspective and why it happened. I'm sure they didn't mean for it to come off as rejection, but it still does, and I have had to heal from that.

I asked the Lord why I desire intimate relationships (intimate as in spiritual and emotional intimacy) with women in leadership? Obviously, it's because that's what I didn't have when I was young, and I needed that nurturing. It was a void I was trying to fill.

So I was always hoping there would be these women in my life and praying that the Lord would send them to nurture me through that. Well, guess what? He did. Then it's like the people that I trusted to nurture me, poured into me for a season, and then they would all leave because I *still* didn't know how to get that need met. I was actually wanting to be nurtured, but without realizing it, I pushed away the very people the Lord had brought to me.

It was twofold. There was some fault on their end, and there was some fault on my end, and I just love them so much anyway. Hopefully, they love me too.

I've had two women in my life that have never left, and they see the woman that I am today, and they love who I am. I love who I have become. I'm so proud of myself. I want each of you to get to the point where you can just say, "I'm proud of myself," and truly believe it.

Once I got the revelation and understood that I need to be nurtured, I asked the Lord what I should do to learn how to get that need met in Him. The strategy was for me to fast, food and drinks—the creamy drinks like coffee with Half & Half—all the things that are rich, bold, and make me feel good.

When I'm seeking comfort, I cuddle up in a blanket, get my coffee, get a book, watch a John Paul Jackson teaching, a Joyce Meyer teaching, or whoever I feel led to listen to that day, and I feel comforted. Well, instead of coping in that way, I wanted to fast those things that made me feel comforted and ask the Lord each time what He wants me to do to meet that need.

I can remember being younger and just longing for a hug. I would pray that the Lord would put someone in my path to give me a meaningful hug that day. Obviously, physical touch is one of my main love languages. One of my pastors actually recommended that I get a massage regularly because it's just someone who's taking their time to focus on me, since I receive love through physical touch. I have actually done that my whole life since she made that suggestion, as often as I am financially able to do it. Sometimes I just ask Robyn.

We need to learn how the Lord wants to nurture us

To do this, we must make space for Him and give Him time to be able to nurture us. This takes discipline because you don't run to your go-to. You wait on the Lord and make Him your go-to, which rewires your brain for good habits. Sometimes in that fast, the Lord would tell me, "Go make that cup of coffee, and I will be there in that with you."

It wasn't a fast where I fasted completely; it was a fast where I fasted my action and asked the Lord how to get my need met in Him. Once I started doing this, all day, every day, quickly developed into a place of peace. I'm learning how to get my needs met in Him. What's interesting is that for the first time in my life, I honestly can say I have completely destroyed depression. If the Lord calls you to fast, it will likely look different than mine. The important thing is to seek Him and obey what He instructs you to do.

As a minister, I help people overcome suicidal thoughts; I do pre-suicide prevention, intervention, and post prevention counseling. I've done all of these for a number of years now in different settings. I can honestly say that now I understand. Because I sought the Lord and became

Chapter 3: How To Get Out of the Cycle

free from depression, I am better equipped as a minister to help others do the same.

Going into this place of peace with the Lord is literally all that matters to me right now. I walked into Whole Foods yesterday, and I just stood there, amazed at how vibrant the colors looked—the bell peppers, the strawberries, the apples, the pineapples, and the oranges. I looked at the trees before I went in and the vibrancy of the green in the leaves. It's not because it's summertime. I have *never* seen colors the way I am seeing them right now, which is invigorating and lively and exciting. This is a snapshot of what living in abundance looks like. I am no longer just surviving and enduring every day; I am thriving and enjoying the process of everyday life.

I pray for everyone reading this to experience transcendent peace. I asked the Lord, "What is this that I am feeling? How can I explain this to other people? I can see it in the spirit, but putting words to it is hard for me." He said, "It's "transcendent" peace.

I looked it up, and it simply means superior; above and beyond. It means from another perspective that is not of this world; one that is above or superior to this world.

I said, "Lord, this sounds like the peace that surpasses all understanding." Robyn looked up what surpassing means, and it's the same thing as transcendent!

I'm gonna tell you something that's very valuable and very important to me. I have asked the Lord to help me be more clear, more concise, and more defined in how to simply put this information out there for each of you to grasp, and in a way that you will love it, receive it, and walk in it. We are all called to heavenly visitations. We are all called to being in heaven first and on earth second.

We get a lot of questions like: *Are heavenly visitations or translations from God*? Some visitations are, and some of them are not. You can also get translated, taken, and led astray by demonic spirits. But yes, God does give His people heavenly visitations, and He would like to do that for you!

The Pathway to Transcendent Peace

Here's my perspective as a seer, which is my primary gifting: I think it's beautiful. I'm so thankful for the experience when people tell me about a trip to heaven. I am *more* impressed with the relationship; that I grow with Jesus from the experience, and how it changes me physically, spiritually, internally, three-dimensionally, and DNA wise so I can be a light and help other people to change in that area.

Take Kevin Zadai for example. When he was taken up to heaven, Kevin came back a completely transformed man, and he now goes around changing people's lives for the better. That is literally what Kathi and Kevin Zadai do every day. It's just beautiful; there's so much light in them because of that experience.

When you experience heaven, you learn that it's more valuable to live seated in heavenly places with Jesus, at the right hand of the Father. The Bible says we are seated in heavenly places. When you can pursue looking at the world from the perspective of being in heavenly places, *then* you can bring heaven to earth as we're commanded to do. This is the will of God for us.

But we can't bring heaven to earth without first being a part of heaven and understanding that's where our identity is—that's where we live—then walking it out on earth and bringing it to earth. But here's the thing; we are a three-part being.

We are a spirit; we have a soul; we live in a body

Think of your spirit as a circle at your core; it's the core of your being. Our soul encompasses our spirit. Our spirit is encompassed by our soul, and our soul lives in our body.

Because I am a seer, when I'm coaching, I do a lot of it from a seeing perspective. I don't say that; it's just how I operate. I see some people who are shining with light. It is similar to the sun, which has rays of light coming out of it. But some people don't have that light. Others have the rays of light, but there are gaps in between the rays.

It's not darkness; it's being void of light if that makes sense. I don't see evil coming from them, I see them void of light. If you know anything about earth science, you know that darkness is just the absence of light.

Chapter 3: How To Get Out of the Cycle

Any time light penetrates the darkness, it doesn't even have anything to fight because darkness is not matter; light just fills the room. Light is a substance that has mass that fills the room; then it just takes over.

I asked the Lord, "What is it that I'm seeing? How do we get a full light sphere around this person, spreading out to touch other people"

If you think about it, this is how shadows healed people in the Bible. The light would emanate out, and the light contains matter. The light contains mass, so when it goes out from you and touches someone, it literally changes the structure from which they're operating. It changes their cellular makeup. What the Lord showed me was that we have a spirit that's encompassed by a soul. Our spirit is pure and beautiful and full of light when we are born again and walking with the Lord.

That's why the Word says not to harden our heart (Psalm 95:8). That word for heart is "psuché," which actually refers to the mind, will, and emotions—our soul.

When we allow our soul to become hardened, it results in physical ailments like atherosclerosis, which causes hardening of the arteries, and plaque formations, which are hardenings in the brain.

We will prosper and be in health as our soul prospers (3 John 2). It's pretty simple. If we harden our heart—our soul (psuché)—that hardness gets thicker and thicker, and it will prevent the light of our spirit from penetrating our soul. This will also affect our body.

When I started seeing colors in a new way, I asked, "Lord, what is going on? Will You show me spiritually what is allowing me to be able to do this?"

I literally saw, in the spirit, neurons firing back and forth throughout my body, creating new pathways, and making my nerve endings come to life. What do nerve endings do? They help us feel, see, and hear; they help us with our senses. So all of those brain cells were forming new paths and new brain cells to come alive. It is possible to create new pathways and rewire the neuropathways in our brain.

The Pathway to Transcendent Peace

A sign and a symptom that you may be struggling with hardness of heart could be tingling or numbness in your body, especially nerves in your peripheral nervous system.

When we begin to allow the Lord to soften our heart by trusting Him—trusting that He is always good—and allowing Him to be our Wonderful Counselor, we will have a softer soul that will allow the light to penetrate it, which actually brings healing to our body. That is scriptural. I want everyone to know this abundant life that I have inside of me. It's for you too!

I told everyone in our Sunday night church group that it's almost as if I am grieving all those years of struggling to be alive, to feel alive. Yes, I know the truth of the Word of God, but to feel it, live in it, and learn how to just *be*, is something that I was never really good at.

It's something that I've always strived for, but now I realize there are so many scriptures that tell us to pursue peace. We are not advised—it's not a suggestion—it is Scripture that tells us to do so. Too often, we are busy pursuing defending ourselves.

Let me emphasize that we need to deal with trust issues as they arise—instead of letting them pile up—so that our heart doesn't get hardened. We need to take time and allow the Lord to nurture us in the way He wants to nurture us. When you start doing this, you hear the voice of God more clearly. From the perspective of a seer, it's almost like I can see my soul from a higher vantage point, and my spirit is watching. I can see when an external stimulus is going to come at me. This gives me the opportunity to prepare to respond to that external stimulus, which is really an attack. This is one the benefits of being seated with Christ in the heavenly places.

When you get comfortable doing this:

- You will realize that everything external is not worth bringing imbalance to your internal state of being
- You will regain control of your life
- You will begin to trust yourself again

Chapter 3: How To Get Out of the Cycle

- You will have self-control with eating, with your attitude, with everything

When you know the peace of God, it hurts your heart to have a negative attitude because *you're* causing yourself to go outside of that place of peace. It's why thankfulness and gratitude in every situation are so powerful.

I exhort you to speak positive affirmations over yourself every day. Like Joyce Meyer said, "I may not be where I want to be, but thank God I'm not where I used to be." It's very simple. Here are a few things that will help you to stay in a place of peace.

Don't "should" on yourself

Don't shame yourself. When we shame ourselves, we fall into a negative cycle and fall into people pleasing because we feel like we're not good enough. Don't even allow the cycle to begin.

Meditate on the fruit of the spirit that you desire to have

Meditate on the traits of the Holy Spirit that you really want to operate in and be known for. I encourage you to meditate on those because what you hang out with, you become. What you spend time doing, you become.

Recognize that we can't control others—only ourselves

When you do this, you will be empowered. You will rise above and beyond any of the external stimuli that may come at you.

You will develop *self-trust* through these self-control and discipline exercises, and knowing that you're going to make the right decision each time.

The Pathway to Transcendent Peace

It's important that we ask God to help us understand when we're feeling out of control. What's interesting is that some people mask this by numbing their emotions and not talking about them.

Again, hardness of the heart leads to numbness in the body.

When we refuse to talk about our emotions, it's actually another way of being in control. This is because you don't want to confront what you feel you control—your emotions. "Back door control," is what I call that. It's important that we ask God what expectations we have for ourselves that are unrealistic?

We have a book called *The Character of Christ,* in which we really go in depth in terms of getting your needs met in Christ. We encourage each of you to get that book if you haven't already.

Ask God if there are any expectations we have for ourselves or for others that we need to lay down at His feet and never pick back up again. What are some more realistic expectations? Sometimes this is a process of recognizing what we expect of ourselves and others now, and then recognizing, "This one's not healthy" or "This one's too much." Then we scale that down to, "What is realistic for me to expect today, and what is causing me stress that I never needed to experience?"

Once you realize this, it is freeing. You have to forgive yourself for expecting so much of yourself. You are perfect and beautiful! I say *"perfect"* in the eyes of God. You're beautifully and wonderfully made, exactly as you are, without accomplishing anything. Just by being *you!* If you're someone who struggles just to *be*, this message is for you.

God gives us a very clear direction on how to overcome this.

When we pursue peace, the Lord pursues what we're doing. He always meets us where we're at and helps us to see and understand that.

If you are reading this today, and you don't know Jesus as your Lord and Savior, but you've been looking for that place of peace, Jesus's arms are open wide! He is *lovesick* for you! He is passionately pursuing you for exactly who you are and exactly where you're at right now in your life.

Chapter 3: How To Get Out of the Cycle

If you are a Christian, but you want that refreshing of the Lord—that renewal of hope, love, and peace in your relationship that surpasses all understanding, that is *transcendent*, that makes you feel reborn again—I pray this for you too:

I pray right now in the name of Jesus that you would accept that Jesus Christ died for your sins, and that He took them all upon Himself as He became a curse for us and our fallen behavior. He died, He is risen, He sits at the right hand of the Father, and He will return one day.

I speak the Holy Spirit into you, and I release the Holy Spirit to do everything He would like to do in your life to make you feel rebirthed, awake, and alive. To open your senses—all five of your senses, and your sixth sense—your spiritual sense. All of your senses as never before.

I pray that all depression would be eradicated from you right now, in the name of Jesus, and that your body manifests signs of healing where you may not have had healing before. Amen.

Chapter 4: Self-Sabotaging Tendencies

I created this teaching with the help of the Holy Spirit. I believe that it's very simple but will be very impactful and relatable for each of you. I personally believe we all have codependent tendencies that we must fight away, and then make sure that we are grounded in our belief system—grounded in God and His Word—in order to maintain focus and not fall back into any of these tendencies.

A lot of these tendencies you see will go along with our book, *Expel the Jezebel In Me*. It would be beneficial for you to get this thirty-day devotional, which helps to prepare the way for healing; but we're gonna go a little deeper even than that.

My definition of a codependent person is one who continually operates in behaviors that should be strictly for survival.

So what does that mean? You can pause here and just think on that and probably come up with what that means by yourself.

When we are in survival mode, behaviorally, we believe that we need to do something to prevent pain. We believe we need to prevent trauma, we need to prepare, and we need to hype ourselves up and create defense mechanisms that come up when we believe our well-being is at risk. We will do whatever is necessary to ensure that we survive—whatever the cost.

This is naturally for good reason. I mean, we have to have survival mechanisms at times, but it becomes a codependent issue when we *stay* in that survival mode, and we continue to operate using unhealthy habits. We can go a lot of places with this, but I'm gonna stick with our relationship with ourselves and our relationships with other people.

When we're in survival mode, we get distracted from hearing the truth of God

Scientific studies show that when you are in a crisis situation, and you're forced into survival mode (or you *think* you're being forced into survival mode), you actually make decisions that are *four* grades lower than the education you have. If you have a high school diploma, you will operate and make decisions at the level of a junior high school student when you're in a crisis situation. You do the math for the level of education you have.

We want to help people get out of survival mode, and the pattern of slipping back into it, so they can think optimally, hear the Lord, make clear and sound decisions, and not react to everything they encounter.

When we're in survival mode, we typically react to the things going on around us instead of responding to them

Here's a practical example: you're busy, you have a lot to accomplish at work, and it seems like everyone and everything tries to interrupt you, and you have a meltdown. Most of the time, when we're not in survival mode, interruptions would not cause a meltdown. They would just cause us to take a step back and say, "I need to change my plan and set more realistic goals for today because, due to the circumstances, my current goals are not going to be met."

People fall into survival behaviors when they have never developed other options for dealing with overwhelming circumstances. We know this; I'm just putting words to it to help give you language to use in communicating this in your relationships or as you minister to others.

Chapter 4: Self-Sabotaging Tendencies

Some examples that cause people to stay in a place of survival are:

- Abandonment issues that have not been dealt with
- Rejection that has not been dealt with
- People pleasing
- Seeking approval

Again, the *biggest* thing that summarizes all of these issues is a *fear of disconnection.* The fear of disconnection is what keeps us in a cycle of being in survival mode in relationships.

We are inherently created to have meaningful connections with our Creator and with those the Lord places in our lives and around us. We have a deep desire to be in constant, meaningful, valuable, deep connection with at least one other person. When we don't have that, we continually seek it, and we can't understand why we don't have it. So sometimes we try to take control of our relationships to make that happen.

Self-Sabotaging Behaviors

You get mad when you can't stick to your routine, or the opposite; you're out of control and have no routine

Think of Jesus and all of the things He did that we read about in the Bible. He never performed a miracle without being inconvenienced. He never just set out to do the miracle. He was doing something else and got interrupted, so then He changed His plan and went with the flow to meet the needs of the people. Not once will you see Him get irritated because He had to change His plans to go meet someone's needs.

We accuse people

Let's take a romantic relationship, for example: someone who is constantly looking for reasons to accuse their spouse of cheating on them. When someone is looking for evidence of cheating—constantly

The Pathway to Transcendent Peace

searching the phone, constantly searching the computer—they are pre-emptively accusing their spouse so they can avoid the pain of finding out later.

There are times in marriages where things like that happen. Once that happens, you have to be healed from that to have a resolution, and then begin to build trust again with the person so you can move on without it consuming your life. That's just one example, but we can accuse people of all kinds of stuff.

Another big thing in relationships is that we accuse people of doing what they used to do, even when they're no longer doing it. We don't give them a chance to grow.

The other day, I was talking to Robyn. All of these letters for Asher's toy puzzle had been thrown around the toy room, but only the puzzle had been picked up, and the pieces were in the toy box. If you know toddlers, you know that if you leave something in their toy box, it's all going to get lost and you're going to have to buy a new puzzle. It was a big expensive puzzle.

So I was like, "Robyn, could you not just pick up the puzzle pieces?"

But, in reality, Asher (my three-year-old at the time) is the one who threw those all over the room. So I'm thinking of Robyn's *past* of not picking stuff up, instead of assuming that it wasn't him. Or even instead of just asking if he remembered to do this or assuming the best, I went ahead and accused him.

A healthy example of this happened when we lived in our old house. I can't tell you *how* many times I asked Robyn to put his laundry in his laundry basket. Every married couple that's reading this has this issue, so I don't feel bad. Finally, he started doing it. If he was in the bathroom, and the laundry basket was in the bathroom, and that's where he took his clothes off, he'd put them in there. That's progress.

I walked into the bathroom one day, and there were clothes lying *beside* the laundry basket; the laundry basket was empty. And I'm like, *really?* So I made it a point to be mindful. I took a moment and asked myself about all of the scenarios that could happen in this instance: let me *ask him* instead of *accusing him*.

Chapter 4: Self-Sabotaging Tendencies

Well, I asked him, "Did you know you put the laundry next to the laundry basket and not in it?" *Instead* of asking, "Why didn't you do this again?"

He said, "To be honest, I just turned, and I threw them over there. I thought that I made it in, but I didn't know that I had missed." That's an example of how using **mindfulness** and **staying in that place of peace** can help you hear clearly what steps to take to move forward and not assume something about someone. Most of us at some point exhibit codependent tendencies.

When we are in survival mode, we try to defend ourselves

We try to defend ourselves because we're doing eighteen things at once. We have several priorities that we're trying to reprioritize in the crisis, and we can't get everything done that we want to get done. So we're already feeling like we're not good enough, which is an issue that you have to address, or it will manifest in your life during times of crisis or transition. Whether it's expected or not, it still has the same effect.

We go into defense mode, "I'm doing the best I can, don't ask me to do anymore." Then we start getting critical of others that they are not doing enough. You feel like it should be done, but you can't accomplish it, so you blame shift to make other people accountable for something that *you* were supposed to do.

I will give an example of this I recently witnessed. We were in line at our local coffee shop one day, and the person taking our pay for the coffee yelled at her trainee in front of us for forgetting my latte. Then she proceeded to apologize to me and complain that the person that was supposed to make my latte was in training.

I tried to tell her that it's not the trainee's fault. It was *her* fault for not being a leader who is helping her but a leader who is blame shifting. When you have someone in training, *they are in training.* They deserve grace; they deserve to be nurtured in that training, not critically blame shifted because you didn't do your job as a manager. She shut the window on me, and I had to drive away without finishing what I was saying. She was clearly in survival mode herself. It's important that we get healed so our interactions with those around us will be positive, and we can help others get healed.

Having anxiety instead of embracing the waiting period when there is a vulnerable situation at stake

Not everyone who does these things is codependent. These are just some codependent behaviors that can become an issue if you clump a few of them together and see them consistently operate in someone's life.

Consider waiting for the results of a test after you have gotten a biopsy to see if something is cancerous. How would you respond? You can learn a lot about a person while they're waiting. Experiencing anxiety can be normal; it's normal during that situation. But reflecting on *how we respond* to that could show us areas in which we may need growth, such as faith and discipline. It's okay to sometimes not have the answer. Lean into God, and tap into the peace that He has made available to you. As you read this book, you will receive the skills to do this!

How about waiting to hear back from a friend after you just had a difficult conversation with them and confronted an issue? You don't know how it's going to play out. Or asking your pastor for help and waiting to see if they're gonna make the time to help you? Or waiting for your spouse to get home to tell him you're pregnant? There are so many vulnerable situations; and we can see a person's character in those situations based on how they respond during those times—their stability in the Lord, and their self-control (which is a fruit of the Spirit that we all need to develop).

Do we give in to anxiety and go into things assuming the worst, complaining, having a panic attack, or fearing that the relationship is over? Do we make accusations in our head before we really know what happened and actually see the results? If so, that's a codependent issue.

We have issues that arise in us because of hurt from the past. There have been times when we have trusted people with our emotions and what we were going through; we trusted them to be good human beings. No one expects their spouse to cheat on them, but then when something

Chapter 4: Self-Sabotaging Tendencies

negative happens, we do not fully take the time to heal and allow ourselves to be nurtured in the healing process for the negative thing that happened. So we turn to behaviors to try to control the relationship to get the outcome we want, because last time we didn't control it, and it didn't work out the way we wanted it to.

This happens because of abandonment that people have experienced, which can result in rejection and/or fear of disconnection. Then people have hope differed or trauma from a painful or non-loving encounter with someone. When we have that, we can gradually slip into survival mode in our relationships and constantly react out of fear for our wellbeing being at risk. Thus, we don't allow any time to nurture ourselves or any room to grow and enjoy the process. This becomes a habit and second nature, instead in taking control of our actions, being mindful of the things we allow ourselves to think, operating in self-control, really being realistic of what's going on, and not being dramatic or exaggeratory.

We are continually on guard, which raises our blood pressure, raises our heart rate, raises our cortisol levels, can cause diabetes, and so many more issues. Continually being on guard for long periods of time—to keep our stress levels where they should be—turns into control. Most often, we don't realize we're being controlling.

For example, someone cut you off on the road and you're yelling at them when you know full well they can't hear you, and you're not going to accomplish anything. It is irrational to get mad at someone who does something to you while driving. You just need to forgive them and trust that the Lord will give you justice because what you have to say will not change their circumstance, situation, or how they act or respond. Maybe it was an accident. You don't have all of the information. Maybe they got defensive and were trying to protect themselves because they made a mistake. In these situations, we rarely have all of the details. There are many instances in our lives when we try to take control instead of being mindful and responsible for our self-control.

How do we get out of this cycle? We must learn to see ourselves, and the world around us, with eyes of trust and from a place of peace. It's easier said than done, right? I'm gonna give you some strategies.

The Pathway to Transcendent Peace

We see the world through shattered and broken lenses, and we can't see clearly through that window, which means our vision is skewed. Our vision of the future is skewed. There are sticks and stones—hurtful words from the past that have traumatized us. This prevents us from being able to see things clearly and from an unbroken perspective. Most would say that there's no hope for them, that we need to close the curtain, that they'll never get better; but I say that the sun can still shine behind a closed mind.

When we give our mind to Christ, we open ourselves up to thinking like Him—then we will have the mind of Christ (1 Corinthians 2:16). We get the opportunity to lay down all of the hurt, all of the pain, and all of the trauma to receive a renewed mind. It's a *promise* that He has given to us.

There's a battle to remain peaceful, and that battle takes place in the mind. God gives us strategies for that. It would be really helpful for each of you to get the workbook, *Battlefield of the Mind,* by Joyce Meyer, to help you learn how to do that.

We must acknowledge our old behavior

The first step to realizing that we have an issue is to acknowledge the issue once the Lord has brought it to our attention. We die to it; we reject the behavior, we surrender it to the feet of Jesus, and we give our life to Him so we can have abundant life. Only then can we get the fullness of life that Christ died to give us.

We learn to recognize when we continue to operate in survival mode versus getting back to reality after a crisis. We deal with trust issues as they arise, instead of letting them pile up. If you have trust issues (which most of us have), but you see that it's a mindset that's preventing you from moving forward into fulfillment, it is very important to examine the times in your life that you felt abandoned. Journal those thoughts. Address all of the feelings that are associated with that time. Ask the Lord to walk you through forgiveness and give you peace.

I had a conversation with a client today who told me Kat Kerr says that if you can't feel the forgiveness, you should "will to forgive." I

Chapter 4: Self-Sabotaging Tendencies

agree with that to some extent. You forgive as many times as it takes until you convince yourself that you believe it. That is a spiritual warfare tactic, but there's also another level to that, which is recognizing and acknowledging any feelings that are associated with that trauma.

They could be dealing with abandonment issues and saying, "I forgive them for abandoning me," but don't forget that our soul has trauma that needs to be healed as well. We need to encourage them to say things like, "I forgive you for making me feel this way when you abandoned me." That will lead to better results.

Many people have guilt associated with abandonment. They may feel like it's their fault. They may be afraid they're going to continue to perpetuate the cycle because they feel they're not good enough, so why would people stay with them? I just want to take a moment to acknowledge that taking the time to receive healing from God may be difficult for those whose trauma stemmed from their earthly father; however, you will find your healing in the presence of your heavenly Father. I also want to recognize that those who have experienced traumatic experiences from their earthly mother may also have a difficult time receiving healing from the Holy Spirit. I have great news for you though: God is looking forward to healing you and spending time with you, regardless of any issues you feel you may have.

Take the time to receive the healing

So many times we want to give them an answer, and they want an answer to take and run with, which is great; but sometimes, it just takes being in the presence of God to be healed. Sometimes we just have to immerse ourselves in Him, spend time with Him, renew our mind, renew our heart, and allow Him to give us strength again. A lot of us don't like to make time to do that.

We can speak positive affirmations to ourselves and recognize that we had poor behavior in the past, but we must also give ourselves grace and time to work through this behavior pattern. We can't expect ourselves to be perfect, but we can be proud of ourselves for picking ourselves back up and continuing the journey every single day.

The Pathway to Transcendent Peace

Practice mindfulness

This will also help someone get out of the cycle. Mindfulness is simply a topic that has been skewed by the New Age movement, but the basis of it is pure. Stop at scheduled times during the day, and take a minute to ask:

- How am I feeling?
- Am I responding or am I reacting?
- Am I in that place of peace? If not, what do I need to do to get back there? Am I making sound decisions?
- What are my feelings right now?
- What is actually going on?

Take time to be mindful of the reality that you are in and give yourself a chance to breathe and regain your peace.

People will often associate mindfulness with meditation on the Word of God, or on a topic they are really seeking at that time. A good topic to meditate on would be all the scriptures about peace. Pick one scripture and stick with it for a week.

These are really good things to give them as homework. Have them journal how a situation went for them, with the following points:

- What was the progress?
- What were their hangups?
- Where did the issues come up?
- How did they deal with the issues as they came up?

It's very important for us to practice mindfulness, especially when coming out of transitioning from a false survival mode reality when we don't need to be in survival mode.

Chapter 4: Self-Sabotaging Tendencies

We must practice forgiveness with ourselves every time we don't act or behave the way we intend

We need to forgive others because sometimes we feel like it's someone else that makes us operate a certain way—especially if you go through this program and issues arise where you realize that you were abandoned. We need to be sure to walk them through forgiveness of the people who traumatized them, which caused them to go into these cycles.

We cannot control others; only ourselves

When we realize that we cannot control others, we actually get angry that we have allowed another's actions to affect us for so long and take us out of that place of peace—the place from which we should be making decisions. If we're not careful, we can let one person's stupid act take us out of that place and ruin our whole day.

We have to rebuild trust with ourselves that we will do the right thing and make the right decisions. Remember, it took a lifetime of going through trauma to get to the point you're at now.

Chapter 5: Regaining Control Through Peace

The kingdom of God is righteousness, peace, and joy in the Holy Ghost (Romans 14:17). One of the ways you can tell if someone is close to the kingdom of God and knows Christ as their Savior, the Holy Spirit as their Teacher, and God as their Father, is if they have the fruit of righteousness, peace, and joy.

We all know that anxiety is running rampant in the world today; it is a condition that is diagnosed and accepted. Sadly, we learn coping skills from the world; but what's so great about being a follower of Christ is that we actually get real solutions.

Not only do we get coping mechanisms and strategies to stay in that place of peace, but Jesus Himself says, "My peace I give to you." (John 14:27)

Not like the world gives, but the way Jesus gives. He gives us peace that surpasses all understanding. He gives us peace in Him to fulfill us so that our hearts are no longer troubled. We are at perfect peace in Christ Jesus.

> And my God will meet all your needs according to the riches of his glory in Christ Jesus. (Philippians 4:19, NIV)

The Pathway to Transcendent Peace

God gives to us according to the riches of His glory in Christ; He meets our needs, He has met our needs, He is meeting our needs, and He will forever meet our needs.

One of those needs is peace!

We need peace in every circumstance. A lot of people come to us for help to hear the voice of God. Well, a lot of it is being guided by peace.

Let's say, hypothetically, that we have a house we want to buy, or a car we want to buy, or something that we're looking to get into, or a new church that we're going to, fill in the blank. We need to be led by the peace of the Holy Spirit because, chances are, you're not going to open your Bible and go, "Oh, that verse tells me to buy this car."

Now, the Lord can speak to you through Bible verses to go buy a car. The Bible is living, breathing, active, and it is alive. God could use it to do that, but more often than not, we have to listen to the gentle voice of the Holy Spirit who leads us and guides us.

Now I want to share something that the Lord shared with me recently that just blew my mind! I didn't understand it at first; it was almost like a riddle or a parable or something like that. When He spoke to me, I was coming out of a deep sleep, and Jesus said very clearly to me, "The Holy Spirit will teach you more about peace than warfare ever will."

I was like, "What?" That didn't make any sense to me because I thought you had to do spiritual warfare to get into that place of peace.

I meditated on that, and I chewed on it. At the same time, I asked a client what joy means to them. This is a common question that I ask because, if we don't know what joy is, how can we experience it to the fullest, or even have the fruit of it in our lives? It's very important that you're able to define what that is to you. It's not circumstantial.

This client and friend who answered my question gave me all of the things that he or she had to do to get rid of the circumstances in their lives that were causing havoc, instead of actually describing what it is as an object, as a noun, as something we can grasp, or even as an adjective.

This happens all the time; not just with this particular person. I have seen this multiple times; people will say that joy is a lack of negative

Chapter 5: Regaining Control Through Peace

things, or it's a lack of chaos in life—a lack of noise, torment, static, confusion, or anxiety. It's so much more than that!

God wants us to live our lives to the fullest in this perfect place of peace and perfect place of joy. I'm not saying perfect as in you never fail, but it's perfect when you're there. He can protect you in it. That's where He created you to live, move, and have your being. We're not called to lack anything; we are called to live in the blessing of the Lord!

> The blessing of the LORD makes one rich, and He adds no sorrow with it. (Proverbs 10:22, NKJV)

I understand these perspectives. I also understand that it's important to do spiritual warfare. At the same time, though, I think some circles (not all) focus more on spiritual warfare than they focus on teaching what is the actual fruit that we're trying to obtain.

If you wanted a promotion at work, what would you do? You would act like you already have the promotion—you dress the part, you talk the part, you use your time wisely, you're respectful, you're successful—you do all the things you would do if you had already been given the responsibility. Typically, the people that do that are the people that get the raises; they're the people that get the promotions, etc., especially if the favor of the Lord is on their lives.

It's the same principle when we are walking into something that the Lord has called us to walk in—like peace, joy, love, gentleness, humility, patience, kindness—everything.

So when we think about peace, instead of focusing on all of the warfare it takes to get there, let's just act like we're already there. That is a form of warfare, but this is what God showed me: Stop fighting, stop being in survival mode, and just say, "God, I surrender it to You. I cast all my cares upon You because You love me. I'm thankful for everything that I have today. I'm thankful for waking up and taking this breath today. Thank You, Lord. This is a beautiful opportunity to get closer to You today and to love people better."

The Pathway to Transcendent Peace

We can get back to the basics, without being anxious, and really focus on where we're going instead of how to get there. I think there's a lot of golden nuggets in that.

If we put ourselves in a place of peace that surpasses understanding, we're going to be immovable in the sense that we'll realize when we step out of bounds, so we can just go back into that place.

We build what's called "resiliency."

I really learned what it meant to have what I like to call, "peace resilience," after the last F5 tornado that hit Moore, Oklahoma on our street. Most of you remember that well; if you don't, there's documentary after documentary on it. It was an experience I lived through as a registered nurse—a certified crisis responder.

If we continually put ourselves in this perfect place of peace, then when storms come, we will have the resiliency that we've grown and nurtured through practicing staying in that place of peace. So yes, you can call it warfare, you can call it what you will, but I want to focus on the treasure, the gift, and the end result that you get: a continual peace that surpasses understanding. You can make every decision from there and hear the Holy Spirit much more clearly from that place of peace. It is truly life-changing to put in the work to practice mindfulness, receiving from the Lord, and staying in that place of peace and true connection with Him.

For example, let's say I am struggling with negative thoughts about myself—I can't do anything right, I'm not good enough, I shouldn't be this, and I shouldn't be that. But let's just say, you know what, I want to give it all to the Lord. I choose to walk in who I am in Christ, and I know that I am beautiful, powerful, strong, blessed, highly favored, anointed, called, wanted, appreciated—all of these things. Let's say I choose to do this, and this is where I'm going to live.

Each time we choose to do that and get out of a place of negativity, it gets a little easier. We have milestones and stepping stones, and we say, "No, been there, done that." Our muscles grow a little stronger, and we can go back to that place quicker. That is resiliency.

Chapter 5: Regaining Control Through Peace

Now, resiliency can be changed or affected. How well you have it, or don't have it, is based on your childhood. Whether or not your parents helped you come back from temper tantrums as a child—back into a place of peace instead of urging you on and feeding into the emotions, not knowing how to handle it, or yelling at you and making you suppress them, or ignoring you and not helping you process them at all—determines the kind of resiliency that you have in adult life now.

Of course our parents don't do anything to harm us on purpose, and we believe the best about them. That's another way to stay in peace—choose to believe the best about everyone and everything. That's what we're going to choose to do, regardless of the situation. We release them, forgive them, and appreciate them for doing the best they knew to do. Especially if you have kids, you know it's very easy to make mistakes without even knowing you're making mistakes. It's a gut-wrenching feeling of sorrow, and you have regret that you never knew you could feel. Give your parents grace, and allow the Lord to come in, to re-parent us, to heal those areas in our lives, and show us how to move forward. Allow Him to be your Nurturer.

We want to go back to a place of peace and practice going back to a place of peace quicker each time we step out of it. Why is it so important that we stay in peace?

> Now the mind of the flesh is death [both now and forever—because it pursues sin]. (Romans 8:6)

That is why the Bible says the flesh is at enmity with God. This refers to our psuché—our mind, will, and emotions that operate in the flesh.

> But the mind of the Spirit is life and peace [the spiritual well-being that comes from walking with God—both now and forever]. (Romans 8:6)

It's up to us; are we going to let our flesh rule us, or are we going to take up our cross daily and choose to shod our feet and ready them with

The Pathway to Transcendent Peace

the preparation of the gospel of peace every morning when we get up? It's a daily decision. We lay down our lives every day.

I will say that one of the most important declarations to make every morning is, "I declare I walk in the Spirit and not by my flesh today. My flesh is in alignment with the Spirit, and every decision I make will be guided by the Holy Spirit and not from a worldly perspective or my own selfish desires."

> And the peace of God [that peace which reassures the heart, that peace] which transcends all understanding, [that peace which] stands guard over your hearts and your minds in Christ Jesus [is yours]. (Philippians 4:7)

What a good God we serve!

These are things that we can do when we're at peace. I think we don't stress enough the importance of pursuing peace and the power it carries when we're in it.

When we're in a place of peace:

- We're unmovable
- Our fruit is beautiful
- We're able to bless other people
- We're able to make good decisions
- We are a good representation and ambassador for Christ

We're able to meet people where they're at, and actually love them, instead of being self-centered or unable to see or have compassion for what they are going through. This is not possible if we are not in a place of peace because it becomes about us.

> Turn away from evil and do good; Seek peace and pursue it. (Psalm 34:14)

Chapter 5: Regaining Control Through Peace

I think it's interesting that we tend to take certain scriptures and say, "Wow, we're gonna do this really well." Then we omit other scriptures because an emphasis isn't placed on them when leaders are teaching. So I am taking time to teach on this particular scripture.

> Make every effort to keep the oneness of the Spirit in the bond of peace [each individual working together to make the whole successful]. (Ephesians 4:3)

We all know that when we're in a fight with our spouse, it is not fun to pursue peace with enthusiasm because then we have to lay down our pride, which hurts. It's not fun. But this tells us that we should enjoy it.

> So then, let us pursue [with enthusiasm] the things which make for peace and the building up of one another [things which lead to spiritual growth]. (Romans 14:19)

So we need to stop the chattering, the gossiping, the murmuring, the complaining, the fighting, the arguing, being prideful, and wanting to be right, and edify each other in the process. That is peace and love.

I want to give you good news:

> Mark the blameless man [who is spiritually complete], and behold the upright [who walks in moral integrity]; There is a [good] future for the man of peace [because a life of honor blesses one's descendants]. (Psalm 37:37)

There is good news if we fight the good fight to walk in peace. It pleases God when we're aligning with Him and getting closer to Him because we can't have true peace if we don't have Jesus. We just can't. No matter what god you serve, it doesn't matter. No matter what religion you follow, how much you meditate or do yoga, or whatever your religion calls for, you will not find true peace without the Prince of Peace—that is, the Author of Peace, Jesus Christ.

One of my other favorite verses is Isaiah 9:6,

> For to us a child is born, to us a son is given; and the government shall be upon His shoulder, and his name shall be called Wonderful Counselor, Mighty God, Everlasting Father, Price of Peace. (ESV)

If you are struggling with any type of addiction, pain, anxiety, fear—anything in your life—the Lord wants to be your Wonderful Counselor. The Holy Spirit wants to listen to you, guide you, heal you, nurture you, and do everything it takes to bring you back into a state of wholeness. He wants to love on you and show you how much He cares for you—more than anything, and more than anyone in the world could even fathom.

Once we allow Him to be our Wonderful Counselor, He can show off as our Mighty God. We allow Him to be our Counselor, and He goes and defends us. He shows us that He's a Mighty God and able to be trusted, and then He shows us that He's our Everlasting Father. So He becomes our Counselor, He shows up and shows off for us in the midst of battle, then He shows us that He's always going to do this as the Everlasting Father. This is not just a one-time scenario.

Last, but not least, He is the Prince of Peace. I believe that the Lord had this scripture written in this order for a reason—so we would understand the One in whom we live and breathe and have our wellbeing—Jesus—the Prince of Peace. We allow Him to be our Counselor, our defender, Almighty God, the One who cannot be defeated in battle. We allow Him to build trust in us by being our Mighty God and showing us that He is our Everlasting Father who will never leave us nor forsake us. We start to trust and believe that again, and then we realize that He is our Prince of Peace.

We can have peace in knowing these things.

Chapter 5: Regaining Control Through Peace

The God of peace will soon crush Satan under your feet.
The [wonderful] grace of our Lord Jesus be with you.
(Romans 16:20)

I would also add: peace, love, joy, and the Holy Ghost be with you!

If you are reading this today, and you have things in your life—traumas you've experienced that are causing you to be in a state of anxiety, fear, and the inability to trust God—it all starts with allowing Him to be your Wonderful Counselor.

I pray right now that the Holy Spirit would meet you where you're at, and that He would tear down those walls that are so hard against Him; that He would breathe His life into you and show you how much love He has for you right now. Pour your heart out to Him, and allow Him to be your Wonderful Counselor.

I bind the enemy from saying that you don't hear God's voice or hear the Holy Spirit because YOU DO! His sheep know His voice. If you are not yet one of His sheep, I pray that, right now, you would dedicate your life to the Lord Jesus Christ.

If you are in need of peace today, and you are looking for it, I promise you that Jesus—the Prince of Peace—is the only Way to peace. I can tell you that because of the definition of joy from a psychological and sociological standpoint. The definition of joy is this: you know that you're with someone at all times who is pleased to be with you—pleased despite your downfalls, despite your failures that day, your hiccups in life, and all the decisions that you've made.

Joy is knowing that the Lord is always with you, and He is pleased to be with you. I don't know any other god that would do that. There is no other god that is alive, living to this day, and is pleased to be with you just for who you are. You don't have to earn anything! All you have to do is say, "I believe in You."

If you are looking for peace today, I ask the Holy Spirit to begin to move on your heart right now and in your environment—to give you a leading and an unction to feel the desire to submit to Him as

The Pathway to Transcendent Peace

your Lord and Savior. I bless you with salvation and getting to know the Prince of Peace that will crush Satan under your feet.

If you're already a believer, and you need more peace in your life, I speak resilience and endurance over you. I bless you with peace and joy, and the grace to live in them, in the name of the Lord, and the strategies to remain there. And the understanding of what it really means to be in the peace and joy of the Lord.

Chapter 6: Recognizing and Getting Our Needs Met in Christ

Now that we have opened up the topic of what it means to be codependent, and how that can affect our levels of peace and true joy, we must look at getting our needs met. I pray that if anyone has a need that is getting met in unhealthy ways, they will submit those needs to God and allow Him to show them how *He* desires to meet their needs. We were all created with innate needs. Let's take a dive into some of them now, and how what we are doing to get them met plays a vital role in our search for peace. This topic is also discussed in our book, *The Character of Christ*.

Psychologically, we think that in order to be a thriving individual, you have to have your physical needs met, security needs met, and emotional needs met. There are a lot of ministries that are great at teaching and addressing these, even more so than us. But there are a lot of churches, ministries, and families that really don't like to address the other vital needs we have: emotional needs. It gets messy when you're dealing with emotions, but it is our job as the church to help meet the needs of those in the body of Christ in a healthy way, rather than a codependent way.

My dad worked outside of the home; he worked all the time because he was in an unhappy marriage with my mom. He also had to work really hard to pay the bills. He was the breadwinner for our entire family while being self-employed.

The Pathway to Transcendent Peace

Now that I'm self-employed, I'm even more proud of him for all of the stuff he had to do to raise us. As an adult, I can appreciate that; but as a child, I felt abandoned, in a sense. I had to go through very difficult emotional situations on my own because my dad was at work all the time. Sometimes we did talk when he got home from work, and we would end up talking all night long. Then I had to try to get in bed before my mom knew, and get up and go to work and school the next day.

Even if we try our best and do absolutely everything within our power to give our children a godly childhood, we're still going to fail in some areas as parents. I think that's a beautiful thing because it really helps us to reach out to God, rely on Him, and try our best to follow the leading of the Lord.

That being said, if you have the best parents in the world or if you have parents that were the opposite, this book is still for you because we all have needs that God wants to meet. The Bible says that He has supplied all of our needs. If He has supplied all of them, they are supplied. Period.

As you walk this out, you have to have faith. The Bible says that faith is the substance (or evidence) of things hoped for (Hebrews 11:1). We understand that as being something you believe and expect, even though you can't see it. We must believe that when we have asked God for something because we feel like there's a need not being met, we need to identify it, believe it's going to be met, and work with Him to see it come to fruition in our life.

> And my God will liberally supply (fill until full) your every need according to His riches in glory in Christ Jesus. (Philippians 4:19)

Think about it. He wants to liberally meet your *every* need. We have that available to us; all we have to do is ask.

I carry a lot on my shoulders, and the other day Robyn reminded me, "We have someone that told you they want to volunteer. She's gone through the volunteer process, and she's gone through our policies and procedures, so why don't you ask her to help you?"

Chapter 6: Recognizing and Getting Our Needs Met in Christ

I was like, "Oh, yeah! I forgot I could do that in this situation!" So I had a need that was met, but I didn't realize that all I had to do was *ask*.

Recently, we were teaching on the Hebraic month of Sivan. The archangel, Michael, came in fully geared, standing in our office, and he was ready to deliver miracles to people. He had a host of angels with him that were going to do the warfare in the second heaven to get the miracle from God to you.

But, he couldn't have gone out unless we had spoken out. He would just stand there, ready for commission to be sent out, but he would not go until we spoke for him to go.

One more example: Robyn and I were living in an RV, and he could not figure out how to stop a leak that we had from our hot water faucet, which can be dangerous. It was something that we needed to take care of immediately because it was causing other issues. We were still new to living and learning the RV life, and fixing things does not come naturally to us.

After we tried to fix it ourselves, we called to have someone come out and look at the leak coming from the hot water faucet. No one could figure it out! What they recommended we had already tried.

We were on our way back to the RV from Lowe's after looking for a part, and the Lord told me that He was going to give Robyn a revelation of what to do to fix this. I told Robyn and decided I was going to stop looking for the part we needed, and we're just going to pray.

That night, we were lying in bed, and an angel came to Robyn and kicked him. He was trying to get him up to pray. I told him he should probably get up. I said, "There's an angel trying to wake you up, and you're refusing."

He got up for half a second and went to the bathroom. What he didn't know was that it was actually a divine appointment for him to go to the bathroom. Because I am a seer, I saw that there was an angel with an envelope. The angel handed him the envelope, and Robyn went back to sleep.

Robyn getting up was still an act of obedience in the spirit, even though he didn't know it. Because the angel was summoning him to get up, Robyn got up, went to the bathroom, received the answer, and went back to bed. As soon as he woke up the next day, he had the answer for how to fix the leak. It was very simple, did not cost anything, and took two seconds. God is ready and willing to meet your needs. He already has the staff in place to accomplish it. All you have to do is ask.

Basic human needs that we all have:

- Attention—Notice the good in me
- Affection—Welcome me with all my flaws
- Appreciation—Be grateful for me; tell me I add value
- Support—Carry burdens with me
- Encouragement—Inspire me, instead of criticizing me
- Respect—Acknowledge my worth
- Security—Always believe the best about me

If any of these needs resonate with you, don't be afraid to ask the Holy Spirit to give them to you.

We've already established that Jesus wants to meet your every need liberally. Father God wants to take care of His children. If we desire to give our children what they need, how much more does God want to take care of us?

On the other hand, if you read this and your ability to feel has been closed off for so long that you can't tell which of these to start with, then ask Jesus. He is the Great Physician. He will not misdiagnose you. He can be trusted with your signs and symptoms because He holds the cure. Who better to meet our needs than the One who created them?

Chapter 6: Recognizing and Getting Our Needs Met in Christ

What are some signs and symptoms that we are not getting our needs met? Here is a non-exhaustive list:

- The need for constant hugs and affection (the opposite can also be true; no physical touch at all)
- The need for interaction with others in order to be happy
- You have dreams that you ultimately cannot find or get to your destination
- You often feel emotionally numb or critical (however, this can also manifest physically)

Often, when people are being critical, they're not offering solutions; they're only pointing out problems. Something you will commonly hear among military people is that you don't go to a superior with a problem unless you have a solution. Otherwise, you sit down and be quiet. When you're being critical, you're critiquing something in some way, shape, or form.

To critique, which is where the word *"critical"* comes from, implies that you are saying something in order to bring change of some sort. It's interesting that being critical can be numbing because all you're doing is pointing at something; that's the only way you're trying to deal with this situation, instead of actually finding a solution.

Easily irritated or quick to anger

To quote pastor John Thomas, who is now the head of Streams Ministries International, "Quick to irritation or quick to get angry is not a personality issue; it's a sin issue."

If you're wondering where it says that in the Bible, let me take you to a portion of scripture: 1 Corinthians 6:9-20. When Paul listed things that, if done, would cause us to not inherit the kingdom of God, he talked about starting fights for no reason or being quick to argue (which is basically arguing with people and getting irritated over everything). That is one of those things that will cause you to not inherit the kingdom

The Pathway to Transcendent Peace

of God. When I hear: *you won't inherit the kingdom*, what I really hear is: *you won't inherit the promises*.

In other words, pastor John is saying *don't just blow it off because you believe it's your personality*. I could very easily do that. My personality is to get it done, check it off the list, move everyone aside, and move forward. That is my personality; I'm very driven and headstrong. Whether you come with me or not, I have a goal, and I'm going to meet it. I have to learn to take a moment to remember the people that operate a lot slower than I do.

Some personalities may be more prone to this, but it is sin. The good news about it is that when we *are* getting our needs met, we typically won't struggle in those areas (like anger). They'll be resolved naturally without having to focus on it. You won't have to say, "This is sin in my life; how do I fix it?"

I had a dream a few weeks ago in which I had to repent to the Gentle Shepherd for not being gentle. It's not that I'm not gentle, nurturing, and loving; I think I really am. But sometimes I just want to clean everything up, put it in a box, put a bow on it, move it over, and move forward. That can come off as very rude.

As human beings, we have a tendency to say, "I'm such and such." Or, "This is my family trait." For Robyn, it's the fact that he's from New York.

That used to be an excuse for him for why he could cuss, be rude, and say whatever he wanted—or critique every pizza!

We say it's because I'm this or that, but that's just a cop-out. The Lord corrected him when he said, "This is what you call pizza around here? I'll eat it, but this is not pizza; this is bread with cheese on it." The Lord told him he couldn't say that anymore because it's justifying the old man.

Following are behaviors that may have become normal:

- Stuck in the victim, predator, rescuer cycle and sometimes flip between the three
- Carries shame that says, "I'm not enough."

Chapter 6: Recognizing and Getting Our Needs Met in Christ

- Depressed but doesn't know why
- Has self-pity or wants pity from others
- Gossips often
- Passive/aggressive
- Cries more than laughs
- Often feels like they're on an emotional roller coaster
- Knowingly or unknowingly develops dysfunctional habits to fill voids
- Often feels isolated or experiences seasons of isolation
- Has workaholic tendencies (or the opposite can be true; doesn't do anything)
- Has difficulty standing strong in spiritual warfare
- Experiences frequent infirmity
- Is often in despair
- Is unsatisfied
- Can be controlling and manipulative

Sadly, when we are getting our needs met in unhealthy ways, we are not acting in righteousness. Those who are not operating in righteousness are not only in sin, but will not be satisfied.

> The righteous has enough to satisfy his appetite, but the belly of the wicked suffers want. (Proverbs 13:25, ESV)

It is a vicious cycle that only Jesus can break for us. Thankfully, He is the Way! As I said earlier, my favorite scripture is John 10:10:

> The thief comes only in order to steal and kill and destroy. I came that they may have and enjoy life, and have it in abundance [to the full, till it overflows]. (John 10:10)

You may be asking how to get your needs met in Christ. Here are the steps you will need to take to go from where you are to where you need to be.

Get to know your identity in Christ

Our identity is what distinguishes us from other people and makes us unique. Every person has their own special character traits and personality.

One way to invest in building your identity and confidently living in who you are in Christ is to get into the Word of God and get to know *His* character. The only way to get to *know* someone's character is to get to know (gnosis) him or her. That's experiential knowledge; meaning, you are doing things to experience what it's like to be with Jesus.

Walking in your identity is reconciling yourself to Christ. We are all called to the ministry of reconciliation, but we can't do that until we are assured of who we are in Christ. That means that if you believe you have cancer, but the Word says you are healed, *you have to let go of what you believe and align your thoughts with the truth.* That's what reconciling means.

So it's recognizing the area in which we're not getting our needs met, and saying, "God, I fall on my face before You. I thank You so much for bringing these to my attention. I repent. "Please help me to change." The only Person that can help you change is the Holy Spirit.

That's the difference between this book and a self-help book. You must rely on the Word of God and the Holy Spirit to change who you are in a good way. He will keep the great pieces and reconcile to the Word of God the pieces that are double-minded.

To reconcile means to come into one hundred percent agreement with something. I exhort you to write down anything you think that does not agree one hundred percent with what the Bible says about you. Take the time to pray and work through each area until it is reconciled to Christ. Ask the Holy Spirit to reveal any lies you believe, and then search the Scriptures to find the opposite of each lie you believe—find the truth.

This is work that no one else can do for you. It takes persistence, determination, integrity, and honesty with the Lord. Ask Him if there is

Chapter 6: Recognizing and Getting Our Needs Met in Christ

any area that you have blocked Him from your life. Ask Him to help you to be vulnerable enough to trust Him and let Him in.

This is something that the Lord is really having me focus on right now because people are not feeling safe with God. There's a big cleft of mistrust between people accepting Christ and then crossing that bridge to walk in their reconciled identity. The cleft is unbelief—not feeling safe with Christ. People do not trust that God is truly good.

Be open to receiving the love of God

We must allow Him to love on us! We present our heart to Him, allowing Him to speak whatever He wants to say to us, and just spend time with Him. You can do this through simple prayer, journaling, worshipping with your hands raised or open to receive, and so on.

Seek out discipleship

Notice here that I said "discipleship." I am not referring to the controlling, dysfunctional, Jezebel-like, and co-dependent shepherding movement of the past. I am referring to pure discipleship, where the true intention of the mentor or wise counsel is to raise another up until the one they are discipling surpasses them—and with no ulterior motive.

Ask for help and seek out education on topics the Holy Spirit leads you to, but don't seek a mentor to point out to you all the areas in which you need growth. Odds are, the enemy has already been hounding you about those areas, and you are well aware of them. The Holy Spirit is always available to be your Teacher, and He never has ulterior motives or a hidden agenda. Still, He does also want us to be connected to others in the body of Christ. The great news is that He will never leave you nor forsake you. There is wisdom in seeking wise counsel, according to the book of Proverbs, but that counsel should prove their fruit to you before you choose to get advice or help from them. Know that Jesus has the final say above all else. Your counsel or mentor(s) should be very well aware of this too.

We are the hands, feet, and mouthpiece of God, so there may be seasons when He brings others alongside you to help you reach your fullest potential.

One thing I love that John Thomas teaches as well is that it is the ultimate price and of ultimate importance for every person to be able to hear God by themselves and for themselves. But sometimes, the way people hear from God for their situation is through other believers.

Be intentional about spiritual warfare

It is our responsibility to be mindful of when the enemy (or our flesh) is leading us to get our needs met in an unhealthy way. When this happens, we must immediately abort the plans in the spirit—by prayer—and stop him in his tracks.

The Bible says to take every thought captive to the obedience of Christ (2 Corinthians 10:5). This must happen on a daily basis. The word "captive" literally means to take something or someone as a prisoner of war to the commander-in-chief. Jesus is our Commander-in-Chief. Take it—drag it—to Jesus; you have full authority over it, and it's up to you to put it into submission. Like a prisoner, it must submit to the warden, the prison guards, and so forth.

Intentionally and consistently make good choices

This is a part of having good character. We will talk more about this in the chapter on self-control and discipline. Resolve in your heart that you will remain consistent in seeking God and walking in righteousness. Put on your armor, according to Ephesians chapter 6, and take back all that the enemy has stolen from you. If you realize that you have gone throughout your life without any of these needs being met, just know that operating in unhealthy ways is not your fault. The Lord forgives you for that. But now is the time to inform Satan that you have caught him red-handed, and he must give back seven times the amount of fulfillment he has stolen from you.

Chapter 7: What Is Nurturing, and Why Is It So Important?

I want to take a moment to recognize that we *all* have codependent tendencies from time to time. Some people only use them when they are in crisis, and that's a healthy thing to do when it's for survival. However, when it becomes lifestyle, that's when it is an issue. I want you to be looking for these signs and symptoms of manifestations and behaviors of yourself or those you lead.

I exhort you to give yourself a "peace analysis." Simply ask yourself these questions:

- Do you believe you're in a place of peace right now?
- Are you able to maintain that state of peace? For how long?
- What do you do when you get out of it?
- Are you self-aware?

We need to be able to see where we are in the cycle of peace or if we're completely out of it. We can direct you to a life filled with peace, and we can lead you to a life filled with enjoyment and abundance. Thus, you will be able to fulfill your calling. When you're at peace, you can hear the voice of the Lord much more clearly than when you're not at peace!

The Pathway to Transcendent Peace

Getting to this point could be the thing that changes your life forever. Never discredit taking time to develop in yourself or others these skills. We teach people how to live life, not die trying to live life.

There are a couple of other analyses you can do. When I say analysis, I mean a series of questions that show you where you are regarding this topic.

You can do a career satisfaction analysis or a work-life balance analysis. God does not want us to be out of balance in any area. We need to put God first, family second, and career third. We always want to make sure that we are in alignment with those core values and principles. When we do that, everything else will fall into place.

Spiritual health analysis

Stop here and ask yourself these questions:

- How is your relationship with God?
- Do you believe you hear God's voice?
- Are you close to God?
- When did you first become a believer?
- Are you in the same mindset that you were then?
- Are you on fire for God or is your relationship lukewarm?
- Do you spend time with the Lord daily?
- Have you felt the Lord call you to do something but you are not doing it?
- Are you being obedient to the best of your ability?
- Are you enjoying your time with Him?
- Are you obeying Him because you fear Him or because you love Him?

These are things I recommend getting to know about yourself and those you closely lead.

Also of importance are self-awareness and inner healing. I think what's lacking in the body of Christ is that we have a lot of people who

Chapter 7: What Is Nurturing, and Why Is It So Important?

understand inner healing, but I'm going to be honest, I have had more inner healing sessions for wounds that have been caused by people in the body of Christ than I've had for any other reason. You might feel the same way. It's time that we not only talk about inner healing and stored emotions, but about *maintaining* that healing and growing emotionally and intelligently. This will assure that we can love one another and prevent further trauma from happening in the church.

Yes, you can be instantaneously healed and set free. Deliverance is great, but tearing down strongholds after the deliverance is necessary and vital. The deliverance gets rid of the curse and the demon, but walking it out in everyday life gets rid of the stronghold. That's my call—to help post-deliverance people in the body of Christ walk through that lifestyle change.

If you see yourself, or those you lead, struggling with isolation issues, there has typically been abandonment at some point. With that, it is helpful to ask what is the root of the abandonment. Abandonment creates trauma that actually looks like post-traumatic stress disorder in most cases. Everyone's experience is individual to them. Every single person experiences trauma in a different way. There are similar behaviors that come from it, but the way they experienced it requires us to be excellent *listeners*, to ourselves and to others, in order to be able to heal and help others heal.

It's very important for you to evaluate your relationship with yourself.

- Do you critique yourself?
- Are you hard on yourself?
- Do you give yourself grace?
- Are you proud of who you are and where you are at?

We want to assess two things about ourselves: self-confidence and self-esteem. The definitions of self-confidence and self-esteem are as follows:

- Self-confidence: our belief in our ability to do something

The Pathway to Transcendent Peace

- Self-esteem: our fundamental belief in who we are

Self-confidence is based on ability. To assess your self-confidence, ask yourself these questions:

- Who am I?
- What do I stand for?
- What values and ethics do I hold?
- Where does my authority come from?
- Do I feel safe?
- Am I okay standing up for what's right, even when pressure is put on me by friends, family, or society?
- Can I walk alone in life and be satisfied?

Self-esteem is based on identity. To assess your self-esteem, ponder these questions:

- Do you often find yourself feeling like a failure?
- Do you see yourself as someone that deserves to be respected?
- Are you proud of yourself more than you are critical of yourself?
- Are you content with who you have become, or do you have regrets?
- Do you believe you can add value to any circumstance you are in?
- Do you believe you are truly good?
- Are you able to hear negative comments about yourself, forgive, and let them roll off your shoulders; or do you carry them and react to the comments of others?

It's important that you understand the difference between the two so you can assess whether any of these are areas that need attention. Focus and ask the Father to build you up! HE will do it! You don't have to!

I want to continue to build upon the codependency teaching and talk about resilience. Resilience is essentially the ability to bounce back

Chapter 7: What Is Nurturing, and Why Is It So Important?

QUICKLY from difficult situations without remaining in or carrying trauma—this is my personal definition. This becomes important after reading the previous chapter when we begin to learn and receive revelation about some of the ways we may be operating with codependent tendencies. It is of vital importance for us to learn how to bounce back and flip out of a codependent cycle and into the pathway to peace. There are keys to building resistance.

Forgive yourself when you mess up

This morning, I am writing, but we didn't sleep well again last night. Joseph was up for much of the night, and then I got up with him early this morning. We have nine dogs in the house right now. Five of them are ours, and the other four are fosters that we're training to adopt out. All of the dogs were going crazy!

If you know anything about me, you know that I love and hold dear, serenity and calm. I value them. I also think it's really fun to be loud and fun at times, but I don't want it all the time. I need some quiet. It doesn't have to be no noise at all, just not a noise level of a 10/10. That's when I start to get stressed out, and I have to self-regulate. If I am mindful to do that, I can do it in the midst of the noise. I am ultimately relying on Jesus to show me where He is in the midst of the noise. It is there, making the connection with Him, that I find true peace; and that's where you will find it too.

As always, your home is your biggest battleground and your largest training field. Joseph wanted to be held because he's a little spoiled from having the feeding tube in him for eight months. There were several instances when we had to hold him upright so he wouldn't choke or aspirate. There was a lot that went with that, and every time he would cry, he would choke and aspirate his saliva during a feeding. We would have to jump up and grab him every time he would cry, and sit him upright to make sure that wouldn't happen. That created a bad habit in that every time he would cry, he would get mommy or daddy to immediately hold him.

The Pathway to Transcendent Peace

I was over it this morning! I didn't yell at him or anything, but with the dogs going, and it being early in the morning, Asher woke up being demanding. If anything is sure about my three-year-old, he is me in a little tiny version of a boy. He knows what he wants, and he won't stop until he gets it—which can be a good trait—but it can also be hard on a parent, especially first thing in the morning after several long nights.

I got overwhelmed this morning. I had to draw a boundary, take a moment, and step back because I found myself not caring about their emotions. I just wanted everyone to be quiet. I didn't say I didn't care what he needed, but that's how I felt, and that was the feeling I was putting into the room.

During that time, I let the dogs go out to potty, and Asher was afraid the dogs were going to hurt his toys for whatever reason. He thinks that every time the dogs go out, he has to protect all of his toys. He was running and getting his balls, freaking out, and saying at the top of his lungs, "I don't want them to pop my balls!"

So I had his emotions, which were out of control and unregulated (because he's three), Joseph screaming at the top of his lungs, all nine dogs upset, and me trying to keep the house quiet so Robyn could get a couple more hours of sleep before I had to go to work.

I just looked at Asher and said, "They will not get your balls. They can't pop them because they physically can't pop." Then I continued with what I was doing.

Later, I realized that I was overwhelmed in my emotions and not self-regulating well. I was also not being mindful of Asher's emotions. Because I allowed myself to be overwhelmed with my emotions, I shut down my three-year-old. What should have happened was me leaning into the situation and the uncomfortableness of it, and giving him space to put words to what he was feeling. I could have said, "It seems like you may be scared." Or I could ask, "Why are you reacting so strongly to this? What does it feel like for you whenever I let the dogs out? How are you feeling in this moment, and what can we do about it so you won't have to experience fear next time?"

Chapter 7: What Is Nurturing, and Why Is It So Important?

Rationally talk through it. "I understand that you are afraid your balls will get popped; I would be too if I loved balls as much as you do. But, the soccer ball can't pop from a dog just going outside. Maybe if they're chewing it, but that's not what they are here to do. Next time, we'll make sure your toys are put away, and I want you to know that I'm not going to let the dogs ruin anything that's important to you, on purpose." That would have been a way to handle the situation emotionally and intelligently. I had to come out of that, step back, and forgive myself. That is how this story relates to resiliency.

The other thing that unhealthy behaviors do in our lives is create shame storms or cycles. We tell ourselves, "We should have done this or that. If only I had responded this way instead of that way," etc. Fill in the blank.

Billie Boatwright taught me a long time ago, *"Never should on yourself."* It causes a shame storm, which plants seeds of shame and bitterness toward yourself.

The thing to do is say, "I'm proud of myself for moving forward and not staying in this mess of being frustrated and a victim. I'm going to do better, and we're going to have a good day." The more you do it, the easier it becomes.

Since I did that, we've had a good day. I even told Asher that I was sorry for not recognizing his needs. I looked forward to having a better day with him, and listening better. As parents or leaders in anything, it's really important we learn to not only forgive ourselves, but to apologize to other people.

Shame, if we allow it to continue, will lead to suicidal thoughts. I experienced this in my own life. Shame always makes you feel like you are never enough. It makes you feel like you weren't good enough, therefore, you're not good enough to be here. It makes you feel like you're not good enough for a relationship.

I promise you that you're more than enough, and those are all lies from the devil. When you can see that, you will start getting very mad at how much peace and tranquility the devil has stolen from you.

The Pathway to Transcendent Peace

To build resilience, praise yourself and others every time you see a success

As parents, employers, leaders, and as humans, we tend to criticize and make a big deal about things. For example, I was working for a company at one time, and I was meeting every goal. I was setting new records, and I was beyond meeting what they had asked me to do. However, I had gotten really sick while I was pregnant. It was almost time for me to deliver—it was a breech pregnancy, the cord was wrapped around the baby's neck twice, heart murmurs, bed rest, car wrecks—it was a difficult pregnancy.

Right up until those last three weeks or so, I kept being assigned additional tasks, and I was more stressed than ever. I was still setting records and meeting my goals, but I ended up getting punished for not documenting something the way they wanted it done. They weren't clear about it, so I still don't fully understand it, which is probably why I didn't do what they wanted me to do.

I got reamed for that when I had busted my butt to help that company be able to do business at all. I was basically their first full-time nurse, other than the one who was running the company. I was doing the office management, back office stuff, plus seeing patients. It was a lot, but it was okay. I did it, I was excited, and got reamed for it anyway.

It ended up being a very sad ending at that company when I should have been praised and appreciated whenever I had a success or did a good job. Even showing up with a good attitude is something we can praise people for doing. Having a good attitude is a choice. We could all be feeling terrible every morning, or hate life, or hate mornings, and choose to have a negative attitude.

When we have a positive attitude, it's on purpose. It's a choice we intentionally make. That's something we need to make a really big deal about, instead of the times the people around you don't do what you expect them to do.

We become what is emphasized of us. Be aware of what you're doing and why. Many of us grew up in a childhood home where we were

Chapter 7: What Is Nurturing, and Why Is It So Important?

scolded every time we did something wrong. We are supposed to overemphasize and overreact to the things they do right—the things they do well, that make them proud, for sticking to the routine, or choosing to be helpful in their own way—we want to praise and encourage anything that is positive.

We want to praise them a lot, exaggerate and be intentional about having positive emotions, instead of numbing positive emotions. We typically say, "Oh, good job," as in, "Good performance."

What we should really be saying is, "I'm really thankful you made an intentional effort to have a good attitude today. It changes the environment of the entire office, and I'm so thankful to you for you doing that." That is a meaningful-connection response. Those are the types of connections that we want to make with each other. Sincere connections to Jesus and people will help us to stay in a place of joy.

We need to forgive ourselves, not "should" on ourselves. It is healthy for us to be proud of ourselves for having the ability and desire to want to move forward. Self-esteem is the fundamental belief in who we are. Because of who we are, and the Christ that lives in us, we can continue to get up and try again. Every time we work out a muscle, we develop it more, and it gets stronger. Whenever we exemplify a good behavior, we *become* that behavior. If we're in an environment where we are told we are dumb, stupid, a nuisance, annoying, frustrating, overbearing, hyper—whatever the word over us may be—that's what we become.

We have to be very careful to emphasize our successes. We have to emphasize the success we have in life every day, celebrate those things, and focus less on the negative. You grow what you nurture.

We are quick to talk about mental health diagnoses, but we are not quick to talk about actual mental health. We become what we focus on the most. Our society today is suffering from anxiety, depression, suicide, bipolar, ADHD, disassociated disorder, narcissism, you name it. The list continues.

I remember reading the newest handbook for mental health diagnoses, the ICD-10. I was so excited to learn about what was being discovered and taught about mental health research; because, if I could know that, I could know what to do to prevent these issues.

That's more evidence that we become what we focus on. If it was actually called mental health, then we would be focusing on solutions to these things, rather than the actual diagnoses. It's okay to acknowledge that you struggle with something, but it's more important to emphasize the strategy to overcome it than the thing you're overcoming. That has to do with nurturing. NURTURING IS KEY TO OVERCOMING ANYTHING.

What is nurturing, and why is it so important?

Nurturing is the key to pulling someone out of survival mode. When you nurture someone, you're providing them a safe platform upon which comes all creativity and vulnerability. You literally act as a protector to provide them a safe platform. Being nurturing is being helpful in some way to others who can genuinely benefit from your help.

Nurturers are:

- Skillful and alert listeners
- Caregiving—this can be natural or developed if you don't naturally think of yourself as a caregiver.
- Compassionate—putting the feelings and needs of others above their own. They have the ability to move from their routine and not be frustrated about it.
- Generous—giving of time, heart, ears, resources, food, money—whatever is needed to build a solid foundation. Give because that's what Jesus did.
- Positive—takes time for others, expecting nothing in return

Nurturers:

- Feed others—spiritually, emotionally, and physically
- Go out of their way to help, even when it is inconvenient for them

Chapter 7: What Is Nurturing, and Why Is It So Important?

- Have abundant grace for others and themselves
- Build platforms for people to grow and exceed
- Willingly serve others
- Create a safe place for others to express themselves in a healthy way
- Provide necessities such as food, protection, support, encouragement, and training
- Develop extensive language for communication until the person is understood

If you know anyone that lacks someone in his/her life to nurture him/her, what's really important is for you to take the time to help them discover the nurturing part in them and walk them through a forgiveness prayer. Stand in the gap in place of their mom, dad, teacher, religious leader, or whoever it was that didn't give them the nurturing they needed. Ask for forgiveness in their place, and have them release whoever decided not to nurture them. Walk them through the healing process, and then teach them spiritual disciplines about how to receive the nurturing of Christ and have that peace resilience. If this person is you—once you are at that place of peace, and you're mindful, then you can learn to go from dysregulated emotions to regulated emotions and be nurturing to other people. You can only do that once you find healing and forgiveness yourself and let go of the past.

If you research psychological studies that have been done, you'll find that how we were nurtured determines who we are. If you were not nurtured, you may not be very nurturing to yourself. You likely have a certain level of nurturing for other people, but it stops, and you find yourself wanting to nurture but getting irritated instead.

However, there is hope! We can change that. That's what we're here to do as coaches and ministers.

Very rarely is anger or punishment needed in order to change your situation. Think about it; if anger and punishment were the answer, then we wouldn't have repeat offenders in jail.

The Pathway to Transcendent Peace

They say that developing a habit takes twenty-one days for it to work. I believe it takes longer than that because we also have to practice these in times of crisis to really solidify them in our lives.

Traits of a nurturer:

- Compassion
- Positivity
- Servanthood
- Excellent listening skills
- Ability to hold space for another's emotions
- Ability to protect instead of punish
- Vulnerability
- Trusts God more than themselves
- Ability to get their own needs met in healthy ways
- Makes time for self-care
- Sets strong and healthy boundaries
- Practices grace with themselves and others
- Humility—knows they can learn from another's experiences

At Fireside Grace Ministries, we have a routine. It's not set in stone, but it is something others can expect from us. It exemplifies who we are and how we operate. The Lord has taken us through the fire to train us to help people. He has taught us to be:

- Patient
- Generous
- Kind
- Gentle
- Selfless
- Empathetic
- Healthy
- Encouraging

Chapter 7: What Is Nurturing, and Why Is It So Important?

- Balanced
- Mindful
- Equipped
- Good communicators
- Disciples who disciple

These are all things He wants for you as well. He wants to set you free because He loves you. Then, by His grace, He will use you to minister that freedom to others.

Chapter 8: What Is Meditation?

What is meditation? What does it mean? Is it biblical? Should we be practicing it as Christians? Is it taboo or witchcraft?

Many believers typically shy away from meditation. Because of cultural references, it sounds taboo or like a form of witchcraft that we shouldn't be doing. Remember, the Bible talks a lot about meditation. I did a Bible study on what verses talk about meditation and what the Strong's Concordance number and explanation is for the word "meditation." I dug in to learn what is true about it and what is not. There are perceptions that we can receive from cultures we're in, churches we're in, and groups we're in or near, about the things around us.

There are negative ways to use the word that's used in the Strong's Concordance for meditation, which is *"hāḡûṯ,"* which is the Strong's Concordance 1900.[1]

However, the root word of it is *"Haguth,"* which is 1897. It means to moan, growl, alter, speak, divide, ponder, utter, mutter.

So you can see what meditation is and ponder whether that word used in Strong's 1900 is actually the form of it that's used—a pure form of it. But there are other forms of it in which you can use it to devise plans of the enemy—to think about things that are negative.

---

1. James Strong, "1900, hāḡûṯ," Strong's Hebrew: 1900. תּוּגָה (Hagut)—meditate (Bible Hub), accessed June 19, 2023. https://biblehub.com/hebrew/1900.htm

Just like everything we teach in biblical dream interpretation, there's always a positive and a negative connotation to a dream symbol or word. In this instance, there are some pretty demonic religions that believe in meditation.

Typically, the people doing this don't understand that it's demonic. I say typically because there are also those who know exactly what they are doing. What it comes down to is this:

1. What is your motivation for doing it?
2. What god are you seeking when you are meditating?

Most of the time, meditation is focused on some type of religious belief. If you are doing something that is meditation-led, and it's not to Jesus specifically, then it is most likely to another god (a demon).

The importance of being intentional

When I started to learn how to meditate, I didn't learn that it was the word, "meditate." I learned that it was "worship." For us to set aside time every week, multiple times a week, intentionally focusing on the Lord, is worship. If you think about the importance of being intentional, that really ties into the characteristics of meditation.

Here are some thoughts on meditation:

For most of us who have experienced the righteousness, peace, and joy of the Holy Ghost in worship, we've gotten past our intellect—our logical way of thinking—and we have become relaxed, emotionally and physically, which allows the Lord to speak clearly to us.

Some call it meditation; other religions call it different things; but as Christians, we really do meditate. We just call it things like "worship" and "study."

Meditation for a Christian is not a passive activity. As opposed to meditation in Eastern Religions, our meditation requires us to be mindful as we focus on a particular object, thought, or activity (in this case, it would be characteristics of the Holy Spirit, Jesus, God, or Scripture).

Chapter 8: What Is Meditation?

This helps to train our attention and awareness in order to achieve a mentally clear and emotionally calm and stable state.

That is what the Bible tells us to do! It tells us to cast all of our cares on Him and be thankful. That is a form of meditation.

You do want to be careful how you go about meditating. Like I said, if it's not specifically worshipping Jesus, and they don't talk about Jesus, it's most likely leading you astray. Even if they don't say it's to a particular god, the origin of it most likely is.

How do we meditate? Where does the Bible tell us to meditate?

> This Book of the Law shall not depart from your mouth, but you shall read [and meditate on] it day and night, so that you may be careful to do [everything] in accordance with all that is written in it; for then you will make your way prosperous, and then you will be successful. (Joshua 1:8)

One of my favorite things I learned from the previous congregation I was a part of for ten years is how to really worship. That radically changed my life forever. The ability to be intentional and fully immersed in worship to Jesus just radically set me free.

I got more deliverance from my personal one-on-one worship sessions with Jesus than I ever got anywhere else. I've gotten more healing from heart trauma and physical conditions from one-on-one worship time—just by being focused and intentional about not allowing my mind to wander during my time meditating on God or worshipping Jesus.

I have gotten rid of anxiety, depression, and all kinds of other things I used to carry. All things you carry, you can get rid of if you spend the time worshipping Jesus! I'm not talking about the kind of worship where music is on in the background as you're going about your day. I'm talking about an intentional, set-aside time, full-body focused, and your mind encompassed by and focused on worshipping Jesus, reading

The Pathway to Transcendent Peace

Scripture, etc. Even just resting in His presence and allowing Him to speak to you—or thinking, pondering, and studying what it is He tells you is on His mind to say.

This is a key to hearing the voice of God. I've had so many people come to us and ask us how to hear the voice of God. The most beneficial thing you could ever do for yourself is to set aside time to worship, meditate, or soak on the Word of God. It should be a specific time you set aside; you're intentional, and you allow God to take away everything that would be hindering you, burdening you, and keeping you from hearing clearly. It is being in a relaxed, calm state. It has physiological benefits as well. There's reduced stress, reduced anxiety, and an increase in calmness, peace, and compassion. This is necessary for you to have and maintain your joy.

It almost has us grow our muscle to stay in what we call the presence of the Holy Spirit. There's a lot of culture out there right now that has great meaning and good hearts that love to usher in the presence of the Holy Spirit. I do believe that there is a Shekinah glory. The Bible says we get to be in that Shekinah glory with God, and we must cry out for that.

I also believe very strongly that the Holy Spirit's presence is in us. Taking time to worship doesn't always necessarily usher in that Shekinah glory of God, but it allows our soul to submit to the Holy Spirit, which allows us to recognize His presence with us more of the time. He's always with us, but the more disciplined we become at being mindful of Him, the more disciplined we become in shutting out all of the thoughts that go into our mind that cause anxiety or cause us to not be calm. Then we will begin to live in the presence of our God at all times.

For example, I had to learn how to worship. When I was first learning how to hear the voice of God clearly and constantly, I would sit with a journal, and I would worship in my bedroom. I had one of those mini, five-dollar basketball hoops attached to my door, and underneath it was a garbage pail. Above it was a cross. I would literally write down everything that came to my mind before I went into worship and when I was in worship. I would write it down, and then I would rip out the paper,

Chapter 8: What Is Meditation?

crumple it up, and throw it into the basket, hitting my target, and leaving it in the trash at Jesus's feet, never to be picked up again.

This was a strategy I used for a few years to help me stay focused. Even now sometimes, when I have so much on my mind but I know that I need to be disciplined and spend time meditating on the Word, I still keep a notebook with me so I can write down what it is the enemy is trying to remind me I need to do. Since I have it written down, I don't have to continue to be concerned that I forgot this or that. I can practice laying these thoughts down and spending time in worship. I remember being so engrossed and not being able to have times when I wasn't thinking anything. I could not study for my college classes without having music on, the TV on, or something else in the background. I started getting less than 100% on my tests, which wasn't like me, and I wondered why.

I started putting this into practice in my college life as well. I began to be okay shutting everything off except what I was focusing on at that time. The Lord gave me a huge revelation of the importance of being totally and completely immersed in what I'm doing. If I'm talking to you, having a conversation with Robyn, listening to my child, homeschooling, or talking to someone on the street, etc. it's about being present and actively listening in everything I do. I really learned how to do that through worship.

I took that concept I learned, and I applied it to studying—being fully present and not allowing my mind to be fragmented because of multitasking. A lot of people say it helps them focus better, but it reinforces a negative behavior and causes you to be overwhelmed all the time. My grades went back up.

This was not something that happened overnight. This was something that I really had to work on and practice. It did take a few years to become good at doing one thing at a time without thinking about other things, and with no background noise.

When I had kids, I had to relearn everything about how to be wholly-in with a lot of activity and noise. It's a very interesting dynamic that the Lord took me through, having to learn one way and then another.

The Pathway to Transcendent Peace

> But his delight is in the law of the LORD, and on His law [His precepts and teachings] he [habitually] meditates day and night. (Psalm 1:2)

There are other religions that turn to pray in a certain direction, or they meditate many times a day. They don't care about the cost; they don't care what people think—workplaces excuse them for it—they make room for their religious beliefs, and meditate several times a day. We should be doing the same thing! What would happen if we did the same thing as Christians? If we intentionally took time to meditate on the Word of God, the law of the Lord, His precepts and teachings, habitually, day and night—think about it.

To meditate is to carefully consider. It is a very intentional thing and requires self-control.

> When I remember You on my bed, I meditate and thoughtfully focus on You in the night watches. (Psalm 63:6)

> I will meditate on all Your works and thoughtfully consider all Your [great and wondrous] deeds. (Psalm 77:12)

> I remember the days of old; I meditate on all that You have done; I ponder the work of Your hands. (Psalm 143:5)

The Feast of Tabernacles is a time when God specifically asks us to remember the things He has brought us through. We tabernacle together as family and friends. It's important that we do these things because remembering what God has done for us, and meditating on them, actually releases dopamine. Dopamine helps build our immune system; it helps prevent brain cell death by remembering things and activating those cells again, and more.

God literally gives us instruction in the Bible on how to prevent diseases. It's just doing what the Bible says, but how can we constantly do what the Bible says if we aren't constantly meditating on it? There's so much to chew on that we want it to become a habit.

Chapter 8: What Is Meditation?

I'm going to give you an example of when the Bible uses the word, *"hāḡût."* Remember, we are talking about the word, *"Haguth,"* and one of the ways that *hāḡût* is translated in Scripture means to meditate, ponder, or muse.

One of the ways the root word *Haguth* is used negatively is in Psalm 2:1:

> Why are the nations in an uproar [in turmoil against God], and why do the people devise a vain and hopeless plot?

Another version says:

> Why do the heathen rage, and the people imagine a vain thing? (Psalm 2:1, KJV)

This is like the word "devise," where they're imagining and thinking about plotting something for evil. We can use thinking and meditating in our heart on the things of God, or we can devise plans for evil that are not praiseworthy, righteous, or notable. We are called to think on things that are notable, worthy, and to be praised, but how much are we really taking the time to meditate on these things?

How do we meditate, and what does that look like?

It must not include things like New Age techniques, mind control, breathing techniques, or brainwashing. It can simply include posturing your mind, body, and humility to Jesus.

It simply means to think upon. God gives us postures we can use in worship. He tells us so many ways we can posture ourselves for Him.

How do we get into a meditative state?

- We lay it all down to Him
- We toss out the things that are on our mind

The Pathway to Transcendent Peace

- We cast all our cares onto Him
- We are not anxious; we are thankful and trust Him
- We can release tension from our body by stretching
- We set aside a specific time with God to do this

Personally, before I met Robyn, I used to make date nights with God, and I would literally just have soaking sessions. Every Friday night, I would put on worship music, turn the lights down low, flip on some Christmas lights or candles, and that aroma—the smells from the candles I liked—would make me happy. Then I would lay down and not write or do anything. I would focus on what the Lord was saying to me.

This allows you to receive from the Holy Spirit. When you exercise discipline and consistency with self-control, you allow yourself to give everything to God. Just being in that calm, perfect peace with the Holy Spirit gives Him an opportunity to pour into you.

Some of my best teachings—some of the times I've reached the most people, seen the most deliverances, healings, baptisms, and all kinds of things—came from those times when I was soaking with the Lord. The times I have been translated to heaven, had open visions of heaven, and visions of different rooms in heaven, all came from being disciplined and having self-control. Make room for God and allow Him to speak to you.

I guarantee that He has something to say to you. He has something to say to you often—most of the time, in fact. We just have to make room for Him and listen. It changes our physical and emotional life; it impacts us to bear better fruit. We become like Him when we spend time with Him.

There are studies that prove that we can literally rewire our brain by meditating on something for extended periods of time. The more we focus on the Word of God, the easier it gets for us to become like the Word because we develop more and more neuropathways that allow us easier access to that particular skill or fruit of the Spirit. It's a simple picture to me.

Chapter 8: What Is Meditation?

Think of a new road being carved out. It's much easier to get from where you are to where you want to be, or where you need to go once the road is paved—but someone must pave the road.

Other cultures or religions make time for it. What if we did too?

That being said, in the final chapter, I have taken the time to list for you scriptures that pertain to peace. I have also included prayers to pray over yourself as you meditate on them. Lastly, I recommend following this book up with another we have titled *Soaking in Scripture*. Many blessings to you as you wholeheartedly seek the Lord, and may you find true peace in trusting Jesus.

Chapter 9: Peace Scriptures for Soaking

God gives us peace

> For I know the plans and thoughts that I have for you,' says the Lord, 'plans for peace and well-being and not for disaster, to give you a future and a hope. (Jeremiah 29:11)

I believe the plans that You have for me, Lord. I know that You have planned for me to walk every day in peace, and for me to have well-being and not be in disaster. I know that You have planned for me a great hope for a great future, and I declare I live in that great hope and in that great future. I remain in my place of peace, knowing this is true about my future. I will not fret the future because of Your words.

> Behold, [in the restored Jerusalem] I will bring to it health and healing, and I will heal them; and I will reveal to them an abundance of peace (prosperity, security, stability) and truth. (Jeremiah 33:6)

The Pathway to Transcendent Peace

Thank You, Lord, that this promise is also for me. I receive Your revelation of abundance, peace, prosperity, security, stability, and Your truth. I declare that I will walk in the revelation of these things that You have given me, and not by sight. I will not get distracted from Your Word, with the help of the Holy Spirit.

> Remember the word which Moses the servant of the LORD commanded you, saying, 'The LORD your God is giving you rest (peace) and will give you this land [east of the Jordan].' (Joshua 1:13)

Father, I thank You in advance, that You have already given us the promised land. We get to enjoy the fruit of living in the land that You promised us, and we don't have to complain or murmur that we are not there. I declare that we live in the peace of the Lord that comes with the promised land that the Lord has given to us. I declare that we are delivered from enemies who seek to devour us, and we live in a place of perfect peace with You; eating and drinking from Your hand, for the rest of our lives, prospering in the land of the living. I declare that we will not stray to the left or to the right of the land that You have given us, but we will continue to pursue and take ground for You, in Jesus's name. Amen.

> Is not the LORD your God with you? And has He not given you rest and peace on every side? For He has given the inhabitants of the land into my hand, and the land is subdued before the LORD and before His people. (1 Chronicles 22:18)

I declare that I will not have anxiety or worry of any kind because I am focused on the fact that the Lord my God is with me. He is greater than all the armies of the earth. I declare the Lord of angel armies is on my side. I declare He has given me rest and

Chapter 9: Peace Scriptures for Soaking

peace in the midst of the battle; I will keep my eyes on Hm and not on the waves around me. I thank you, Lord, that You have given the inhabitants of the land into the hand of Jesus, and that the land is subdued before the Lord and before His people. I thank You that we have the ability to know that we are protected in the land on every side, so we can rest with the peace that surpasses understanding, in Jesus's name.

> For David said, "The LORD God of Israel, has given peace and rest to His people, and He dwells in Jerusalem forever." (1 Chronicles 23:25)

I thank You, Lord, that we get to represent Jerusalem as those that have been grafted in to Your promise and plan. I thank You that You, the Lord God of Israel, have given rest to us, and that You dwell in us forever. We will always rely on You for peace, no matter what season we are in or how old we may live to be.

> Now yield and submit yourself to Him [agree with God and be conformed to His will] and be at peace; In this way [you will prosper and great] good will come to you. (Job 22:21)

I declare that every time we face a temptation, we will yield and submit ourselves to You, God, agreeing with You and being conformed to Your will, so we may be at peace, and that You will have Your way in us. Because of this, we will prosper, and great good will come to us.

> Dominion and awe belong to God; He establishes peace and order in His high places. (Job 25:2)

The Pathway to Transcendent Peace

We come into agreement with this—that dominion and holy fear belong to God, and that You establish peace and order in high places, in our lands and in our families.

> In peace [and with a tranquil heart] I will both lie down and sleep, For You alone, O Lord, make me dwell in safety and confident trust. (Psalm 4:8)
>
> The Lord will give [unyielding and impenetrable] strength to His people; The Lord will bless His people with peace. (Psalm 29:11)
>
> I will hear [with expectant hope] what God the Lord will say, For He will speak peace to His people, to His godly ones—But let them not turn again to folly. (Psalm 85:8)

Thank You, Lord, that we can always have expectant hope, and that You will speak peace to Your people—to those who belong to You—and will not let us turn again to folly that would ruin us. Keep us in a place of self-control, guarded by the Holy Spirit, rolling in our lives and making us aware of when we are stepping out of a place of balance in You.

> For the Lord says this, "Behold, I extend peace to her (Jerusalem) like a river, And the glory of the nations like an overflowing stream; And you will be nursed, you will be carried on her hip and [playfully] rocked on her knees. (Isaiah 66:12)

I thank You, Lord, for these verses that show us that You nurture us back into peace, and that You have given us the resources we need to overflow in this.

Chapter 9: Peace Scriptures for Soaking

Each of them shall sit [in security and peace] under his vine and under his fig tree, With no one to make them afraid, For the mouth of the [omnipotent] LORD of hosts has spoken it. (Micah 4:4)

Because of the tender mercy of our God, with which the Sunrise (the Messiah) from on high will dawn and visit us, TO SHINE UPON THOSE WHO SIT IN DARKNESS AND IN THE SHADOW OF DEATH, to guide our feet [in a straight line] into the way of peace and serenity. (Luke 1:78-79)

I thank You, once again, Lord, that when we do not know the way to peace and serenity, we are guaranteed that because of the tender mercies of God, the Messiah from on high will dawn and visit us. He will shine upon those who sit in darkness and in the shadow of death, and He will guide our feet straight into the way of peace and serenity. Because of this, I will not fret. I will always know that Jesus is the Door and the Way, and He leads us down a straight road into the path of life and peace.

Prayers for peace/declarations of peace

Do not keep silent, O God; Do not hold Your peace or be still, O God. (Psalm 83:1)

May peace be within your walls and prosperity within your palaces. (Psalm 122:7)

Or let him (Israel) cling to My strength and rely on My protection [My stronghold], Let him make peace with Me, Let him make peace with Me. (Isaiah 27:5)

May the God of hope fill you with all joy and peace in believing [through the experience of your faith] that by the power of the Holy Spirit you will abound in

The Pathway to Transcendent Peace

hope and overflow with confidence in His promises. (Romans 15:13)

May the God of peace be with you all! Amen. (Romans 15:33)

The God of peace will soon crush Satan under your feet. The [wonderful] grace of our Lord Jesus be with you. (Romans 16:20)

Grace, mercy, and peace (inner calm, a sense of spiritual well-being) will be with us, from God the Father and from Jesus Christ, the Father's Son, in truth and love. (2 John 1:3)

May mercy and peace and love be multiplied to you [filling your heart with the spiritual well-being and serenity experienced by those who walk closely with God]. (Jude 1:2)

Grace to you and peace [inner calm and spiritual well-being] from God our Father and the Lord Jesus Christ. (1 Corinthians 1:3)

Finally, believers, rejoice! Be made complete [be what you should be], be comforted, be like-minded, live in peace [enjoy the spiritual well-being experienced by believers who walk closely with God]; and the God of love and peace [the source of lovingkindness] will be with you. (2 Corinthians 13:11)

Grace to you and peace [inner calm and spiritual well-being] from God our Father and the Lord Jesus Christ. (Galatians 1:3)

Chapter 9: Peace Scriptures for Soaking

Do not be anxious or worried about anything, but in everything [every circumstance and situation] by prayer and petition with thanksgiving, continue to make your [specific] requests known to God. And the peace of God [that peace which reassures the heart, that peace] which transcends all understanding, [that peace which] stands guard over your hearts and your minds in Christ Jesus [is yours]. Finally, believers, whatever is true, whatever is honorable and worthy of respect, whatever is right and confirmed by God's word, whatever is pure and wholesome, whatever is lovely and brings peace, whatever is admirable and of good repute; if there is any excellence, if there is anything worthy of praise, think continually on these things [center your mind on them, and implant them in your heart]. (Philippians 4:6-8)

I can do all things [which He has called me to do] through Him who strengthens and empowers me [to fulfill His purpose—I am self-sufficient in Christ's sufficiency; I am ready for anything and equal to anything through Him who infuses me with inner strength and confident peace.] (Philippians 4:13)

Now may the Lord of peace Himself grant you His peace at all times and in every way [that peace and spiritual well-being that comes to those who walk with Him, regardless of life's circumstances]. The Lord be with you all. (2 Thessalonians 3:16)

Grace and peace [that special sense of spiritual well-being] be multiplied to you in the [true, intimate] knowledge of God and of Jesus our Lord. (2 Peter 1:2)

LORD, You will establish peace for us, Since You have also performed for us all that we have done. (Isaiah 26:12)

The Pathway to Transcendent Peace

> Seek peace and well-being for the city where I have sent you into exile, and pray to the LORD on its behalf; for in its peace (well-being) you will have peace. (Jeremiah 29:7)

God is Peace

Declare these scriptures over whatever circumstances you may be facing

> For God [who is the source of their prophesying] is not a God of confusion and disorder but of peace and order. As [is the practice] in all the churches of the saints (God's people). (1 Corinthians 14:33)

> For to us a Child shall be born, to us a Son shall be given; And the government shall be upon His shoulder, and His name shall be called Wonderful Counselor, Mighty God, Everlasting Father, Prince of Peace. (Isaiah 9:6)

> There shall be no end to the increase of His government and of peace, [He shall rule] on the throne of David and over his kingdom, To establish it and to uphold it with justice and righteousness From that time forward and forevermore. The zeal of the LORD of hosts will accomplish this. (Isaiah 9:7)

> The One forming light and creating darkness, Causing peace and creating disaster; I am the LORD who does all these things. (Isaiah 45:7)

> But the fruit of the Spirit [the result of His presence within us] is love [unselfish concern for others], joy, [inner] peace, patience [not the ability to wait, but how we act while waiting], kindness, goodness, faithfulness,

Chapter 9: Peace Scriptures for Soaking

gentleness, self-control. Against such things there is no law. (Galatians 5:22-23)

For He Himself is our peace and our bond of unity. He who made both groups— [Jews and Gentiles]—into one body and broke down the barrier, the dividing wall [of spiritual antagonism between us]. (Ephesians 2:14)

Peace through trials

Come to Me, all who are weary and heavily burdened [by religious rituals that provide no peace], and I will give you rest [refreshing your souls with salvation]. (Matthew 11:28)

"For the mountains may be removed and the hills may shake, but My lovingkindness will not be removed from you, Nor will My covenant of peace be shaken," Says the LORD who has compassion on you. (Isaiah 54:10)

"No weapon that is formed against you will succeed; And every tongue that rises against you in judgment you will condemn. This [peace, righteousness, security, and triumph over opposition] is the heritage of the servants of the LORD, And this is their vindication from Me," says the LORD. (Isaiah 54:17)

For you will go out [from exile] with joy and be led forth [by the LORD Himself] with peace; The mountains and the hills will break forth into shouts of joy before you, and all the trees of the field will clap their hands. (Isaiah 55:12)

Then your light will break out like the dawn, And your healing (restoration, new life) will quickly spring forth;

The Pathway to Transcendent Peace

Your righteousness will go before you [leading you to peace and prosperity], The glory of the LORD will be your rear guard. (Isaiah 58:8)

He has redeemed my life in peace from the battle that was against me, For there were many against me. (Psalm 55:18)

Peace I leave with you; My [perfect] peace I give to you; not as the world gives do I give to you. Do not let your heart be troubled, nor let it be afraid. [Let My perfect peace calm you in every circumstance and give you courage and strength for every challenge.] (John 14:27)

I have told you these things, so that in Me you may have [perfect] peace. In the world you have tribulation and distress and suffering, but be courageous [be confident, be undaunted, be filled with joy]; I have overcome the world. [My conquest is accomplished, My victory abiding.] (John 16:33)

Be assured that the testing of your faith [through experience] produces endurance [leading to spiritual maturity, and inner peace]. (James 1:3)

For the time being no discipline brings joy, but seems sad and painful; yet to those who have been trained by it, afterwards it yields the peaceful fruit of righteousness [right standing with God and a lifestyle and attitude that seeks conformity to God's will and purpose]. (Hebrews 12:11)

Chapter 9: Peace Scriptures for Soaking

Instruction to live in peace

Meditate on these and make them as one within you

Salt is good and useful; but if salt has lost its saltiness (purpose), how will you make it salty? Have salt within yourselves continually, and be at peace with one another. (Mark 9:50)

Whatever house you enter, first say, 'Peace [that is, a blessing of well-being and prosperity, the favor of God] to this house.' (Luke 10:5)

And if anyone of peace is there [someone who is sweet-spirited and hospitable], your [blessing of] peace will rest on him; but if not, it will return to you. (Luke 10:6)

If possible, as far as it depends on you, live at peace with everyone. (Romans 12:18)

For the kingdom of God is not a matter of eating and drinking [what one likes], but of righteousness and peace and joy in the Holy Spirit. (Romans 14:17)

So then, let us pursue [with enthusiasm] the things which make for peace and the building up of one another [things which lead to spiritual growth]. (Romans 14:19)

Turn away from evil and do good; Seek peace and pursue it. (Psalm 34:14)

But the humble will [at last] inherit the land and will delight themselves in abundant prosperity and peace. (Psalm 37:11)

The Pathway to Transcendent Peace

Make every effort to keep the oneness of the Spirit in the bond of peace [each individual working together to make the whole successful]. (Ephesians 4:3)

So stand firm and hold your ground, having tightened the wide band of truth (personal integrity, moral courage) around your waist and having put on the breastplate of righteousness (an upright heart), and having strapped on your feet the gospel of peace in preparation [to face the enemy with firm-footed stability and the readiness produced by the good news]. Above all, lift up the [protective] shield of faith with which you can extinguish all the flaming arrows of the evil one. (Ephesians 6:14-16)

The things which you have learned and received and heard and seen in me, practice these things [in daily life], and the God [who is the source] of peace and well-being will be with you. (Philippians 4:9)

Let the peace of Christ [the inner calm of one who walks daily with Him] be the controlling factor in your hearts [deciding and settling questions that arise]. To this peace indeed you were called as members in one body [of believers]. And be thankful [to God always]. (Colossians 3:15)

For indeed you already do practice it toward all the believers throughout Macedonia [by actively displaying your love and concern for them]. But we urge you, brothers and sisters, that you excel [in this matter] more and more, and to make it your ambition to live quietly and peacefully, and to mind your own affairs and work with your hands, just as we directed you, so that you will behave properly toward outsiders [exhibiting good character, personal integrity, and moral courage worthy of the respect of the outside world], and be dependent on no one and in need of nothing [be self-supporting]. (1 Thessalonians 4:10-12)

Chapter 9: Peace Scriptures for Soaking

Run away from youthful lusts—pursue righteousness, faith, love, and peace with those [believers] who call on the Lord out of a pure heart. (2 Timothy 2:22)

The servant of the Lord must not participate in quarrels, but must be kind to everyone [even-tempered, preserving peace, and he must be], skilled in teaching, patient and tolerant when wronged. (2 Timothy 2:24)

Continually pursue peace with everyone, and the sanctification without which no one will [ever] see the Lord. (Hebrews 12:14)

He must turn away from wickedness and do what is right. He must search for peace [with God, with self, with others] and pursue it eagerly [actively—not merely desiring it]. (1 Peter 3:11)

Greet one another with a kiss of love. To all of you who are in Christ, may there be peace. (1 Peter 5:14)

So, beloved, since you are looking forward to these things, be diligent and make every effort to be found by Him [at His return] spotless and blameless, in peace [that is, inwardly calm with a sense of spiritual well-being and confidence, having lived a life of obedience to Him]. (2 Peter 3:14)

Blessings that come from peace/How to get peace

Blessed [inwardly peaceful, spiritually secure, worthy of respect] are the gentle [the kind-hearted, the sweet-spirited, the self-controlled], for they will inherit the earth. (Matthew 5:5)

The Pathway to Transcendent Peace

Blessed [spiritually calm with life-joy in God's favor] are the makers and maintainers of peace, for they will [express His character and] be called the sons of God. (Matthew 5:9)

Blessed [comforted by inner peace and God's love] are those who are persecuted for doing that which is morally right, for theirs is the kingdom of heaven [both now and forever]. (Matthew 5:10)

Leave your offering there at the altar and go. First make peace with your brother, and then come and present your offering. (Matthew 5:24)

Mark the blameless man [who is spiritually complete], and behold the upright [who walks in moral integrity]; There is a [good] future for the man of peace [because a life of honor blesses one's descendants]. (Psalm 37:37)

Those who love Your law have great peace; Nothing makes them stumble. (Psalm 119:165)

Blessed [with wisdom and prosperity] is the man whom You discipline and instruct, O LORD, and whom You teach from Your law, that You may grant him [power to calm himself and find] peace in the days of adversity, until the pit is dug for the wicked and ungodly. (Psalm 94:12-13)

Long life is in her right hand; in her left hand are riches and honor. Her ways are highways of pleasantness and favor, and all her paths are peace. (Proverbs 3:16-17)

Deceit is in the heart of those who devise evil, But counselors of peace have joy. (Proverbs 12:20)

Chapter 9: Peace Scriptures for Soaking

A calm and peaceful and tranquil heart is life and health to the body, But passion and envy are like rottenness to the bones. (Proverbs 14:30)

When a man's ways please the LORD, He makes even his enemies to be at peace with him. (Proverbs 16:7)

Better is a dry morsel [of food served] with quietness and peace than a house full of feasting [served] with strife and contention. (Proverbs 17:1)

You will keep in perfect and constant peace the one whose mind is steadfast [that is, committed and focused on You—in both inclination and character], Because he trusts and takes refuge in You [with hope and confident expectation]. (Isaiah 26:3)

And the effect of righteousness will be peace, and the result of righteousness will be quietness and confident trust forever. Then my people will live in a peaceful surrounding, and in secure dwellings and in undisturbed resting places. (Isaiah 32:17-18)

Oh, that you had paid attention to My commandments! Then your peace and prosperity would have been like a [flowing] river, And your righteousness [the holiness and purity of the nation] like the [abundant] waves of the sea. (Isaiah 48:18)

Therefore, thus says the LORD [to Jeremiah], "If you repent [and give up this mistaken attitude of despair and self-pity], then I will restore you [to a state of inner peace] So that you may stand before Me [as My obedient representative]; And if you separate the precious from the worthless [examining yourself and cleansing your heart from unwarranted doubt concerning My faithfulness],

The Pathway to Transcendent Peace

You will become My spokesman. Let the people turn to you [and learn to value My values]— But you, you must not turn to them [with regard for their idolatry and wickedness]. (Jeremiah 15:19)

And He shall stand and shepherd and guide His flock in the strength of the Lord, In the majesty of the name of the Lord His God; And they shall dwell [secure in undisturbed peace], Because at that time He shall be great [extending His authority] [Even] to the ends of the earth. (Micah 5:4)

Then He said to her, "Daughter, your faith [your personal trust and confidence in Me] has restored you to health; go in peace and be [permanently] healed from your suffering." (Mark 5:34)

He said to her, "Daughter, your faith [your personal trust and confidence in Me] has made you well. Go in peace (untroubled, undisturbed well-being)." (Luke 8:48)

But glory and honor and inner peace [will be given] to everyone who habitually does good, to the Jew first and also to the Greek. (Romans 2:10)

Therefore, since we have been justified [that is, acquitted of sin, declared blameless before God] by faith, [let us grasp the fact that] we have peace with God [and the joy of reconciliation with Him] through our Lord Jesus Christ (the Messiah, the Anointed). (Romans 5:1)

Now the mind of the flesh is death [both now and forever—because it pursues sin]; but the mind of the Spirit is life and peace [the spiritual well-being that comes from walking with God—both now and forever]. (Romans 8:6)

Chapter 9: Peace Scriptures for Soaking

Peace and mercy be upon all who walk by this rule [who discipline themselves and conduct their lives by this principle], and upon the [true] Israel of God (Jewish believers). (Galatians 6:16)

For we who believe [that is, we who personally trust and confidently rely on God] enter that rest [so we have His inner peace now because we are confident in our salvation, and assured of His power], just as He has said, "AS I SWORE [an oath] IN MY WRATH, THEY SHALL NOT ENTER MY REST," [this He said] although His works were completed from the foundation of the world [waiting for all who would believe]. (Hebrews 4:3)

But the wisdom from above is first pure [morally and spiritually undefiled], then peace-loving [courteous, considerate], gentle, reasonable [and willing to listen], full of compassion and good fruits. It is unwavering, without [self-righteous] hypocrisy [and self-serving guile]. (James 3:17)

And the seed whose fruit is righteousness (spiritual maturity) is sown in peace by those who make peace [by actively encouraging goodwill between individuals]. (James 3:18)

But let it be [the inner beauty of] the hidden person of the heart, with the imperishable quality and unfading charm of a gentle and peaceful spirit, [one that is calm and self-controlled, not overanxious, but serene and spiritually mature] which is very precious in the sight of God. (1 Peter 3:4)

I pray that every word that you read in this book will transform you from the inside out. I pray that you find healing and

The Pathway to Transcendent Peace

deliverance from behaviors and tendencies that everyday life tries to guide us back into doing when all we want is to walk in the peace of God and minister it to others. I pray your heart will be mended and every area that has caused you to rely on your own mechanisms to find peace will be made whole. I pray that you will have the desire to allow God to nurture you—that you will find that perfect place of peace through being nurtured and allowing the Holy Spirit to meet every one of your needs.

I bless you with the ability to nurture other people and help them to navigate their circumstances, even the most difficult, and to nurture yourself when you need it as well. I bless you with this: you are worth nurturing; you are wanted; you are needed; you are appreciated; you are respected; you are honored. I bless you as you go out into the world after having meditated on the Word of God, and I bless you with the desire to continue to meditate on the Word of God. I bless you to allow the Word of God to get deep inside of you—so deep that you can't not obey it—so deep inside of you that your automatic response in the midst of a crisis is to respond the way the Word of God tells us to respond.

I bless you with such a life-changing journey of spending time with God that you won't want to go anywhere else. I bless you with the desire to share these peace scriptures and to share with all those around you the power of meditating on the Word of God.

Thank you for reading this book, and thank you for being part of a movement to help every person get back to peace by crushing anxiety, fear, worry, distress, and anger in our land! I bless you in the mighty name of Jesus!

About the Authors

Robyn and Brandi Cunningham are the founders of Fireside Grace, which was birthed to help individuals, ministries, and cities live to their full potential through Christ-based discipleship. Using the gifts of the Spirit, they teach truth to bring clarity to the body of Christ on issues that seem confusing in this modern age. They have a YouTube channel called Fireside Grace Ministries.

The Cunningham's goal to is to guide the church body by connecting the ethics, values, character, and morals of our ancestors into the present and future generations by creatively bringing the wisdom of the past, the wisdom of the Ancient of Days, and the wisdom of our elders into the present—and bridging the gaps of the generations in between. Together, Robyn and Brandi cover topics such as current issues, dream interpretation, learning how to hear God's voice, anointing, slaying sacred cows, and much more.

Robyn and Brandi are ordained under Michael French with Patria Ministries. They have been involved with various areas of ministry for the last ten years and travel full-time, writing, speaking, and leading worship together. They minister very often to families considering abortion, helping them feel safe and supported enough to choose to parent, with a firm belief in the importance of teaching about the family unit. Brandi does professional life coaching and is a dog trainer, and believes that all dogs deserve a chance. The Cunninghams are based out of Arkansas, run an animal sanctuary, and have incredible children.

To contact the Cunninghams, visit www.FiresideGrace.com.

Subscribe to their YouTube channel: Tomorrow's Headlines, Today! https://www.youtube.com/@tomorrowsheadlinestodayfir7975

Other Books by the Author:

The Dream Symbol Guide

Do you ever wonder what your dreams mean?

The parabolic language of dreams has long since been a mystery. Dreams invoke a thirst for supernatural understanding, and oftentimes lead many into new levels of spiritual awareness. With the plethora of dream symbols, dictionaries, and teachers, Brandi and Robyn saw a need for a Christian dream dictionary that would not only give an answer for what a symbol means, but would also give instructions about how to discern the meaning of dream symbols and equip readers to rely on the Holy Spirit to help interpret their dreams.

The Dream Symbol Guide unpacks thirteen different categories of symbols, with hundreds of entries covering many common and unique things that are in people's dreams, along with helpful teaching and perspective from Robyn and Brandi to assist you on the journey of understanding your dreams.

For more information, visit www.FiresideGrace.com.

Other Books by the Author:

The Character of Christ

Character, in its simplest form, is the display of who we are when put under fire or to the test. This is when we see the fruit of who we are shining brightly. The Bible makes it clear that it is important for us to "bear good fruit" in season and out of season. This makes sense because it aligns with the character of Christ. He bore healthy fruit for all to see at all times and persevered through the fieriest of the trials a human could face. He showed us that we, too, possess the ability to remain the same yesterday, today, and tomorrow, despite the trials and circumstances that may arise.

Join us and the remnant as we grow and become strong enough in Jesus to press on through any amount of persecution that is here or may come!

"I am fully convinced that now, more than ever, what the Body of Christ needs more than anything else is the character of Christ."

~Brandi, Fireside Grace Ministries

For more information, visit www.FiresideGrace.com.

Other Books by the Author:

Expel the Jezebel in Me

The spirit of Jezebel is running rampant in our country!

In this day and age, the spirit of Jezebel can be found on our TVs, in our music, in our schools, and almost everywhere you look around you. But what if I told you that the Jezebel spirit could also be influencing your actions from areas in your life where you haven't allowed Jesus to shine His light?

Expel the Jezebel in Me is a thirty-day devotional to help you see Jezebellic tendencies in yourself or others and shine light on the pathway to freedom. Each day presents a different trait of the spirit of Jezebel and how to recognize, expose, and expel it.

If you've blamed someone for being a Jezebel or have been wounded by the label of a Jezebel, this devotional is for you. It is time to get set free, learn the tools, and help others find freedom too!

For more information, visit www.FiresideGrace.com.

Why Choose Life Coaching?

As a life coach, Brandi Cunningham's job is to motivate you and help you develop the skills that it takes to continually stay motivated, even when no ones there to motivate you.

Maybe you don't know your purpose, or your calling. But just because it's not clear to you, doesn't mean you don't have one. Everyone has one!

Maybe you know your passion and calling but are not seeing the results you want because you're only able to halfheartedly devote your life to your calling, all the while feeling social and economic pressure to make money to pay the bills.

I'm here to help you save energy and time so that you can use it more on what you're passionate about, until you can do your passion, FULL TIME!

You see, you're unique. You have been made with skills are passions I do not have, and I need you—the world needs you. I won't just stand by and watch people die inside to depression, suicide, or anger because they had no one to help show them the way.

I'm here to help show you, and help you walk in that way. You can do this! Will you let us help?

Email them at FiresideGrace@gmail.com for more information regarding availability for coaching.

www.ingramcontent.com/pod-product-compliance
Lightning Source LLC
Chambersburg PA
CBHW072038110526
44592CB00012B/1465